Babies through Kindergarten Edition

Published by LifeWay Press®
© 2010 LifeWay Press®

No part of this work may be reproduced or transmitted in any form or by any means, electronic or mechanical, including photocopying and recording, or by any information storage or retrieval system, except as may be expressly permitted in writing by the publisher. Requests for permission should be addressed in writing to LifeWay Press®, One LifeWay Plaza, Nashville, TN 37234-0172.

ISBN: 1415868727
Item 005266980

This book is a resource for both the Preschool and Children's Leadership and Skill Development category of the Christian Growth Study Plan.
Courses LS-0013, LS-0015, LS-0021, LS-0023, LS-0056, LS-0106

Dewey Decimal Classification Number: 259.22
Subject Heading: CHURCH WORK WITH CHILDREN\ CHRISTIAN EDUCATION\ RELIGIOUS EDUCATION CHILDREN

Printed in the United States of America

Childhood Ministry Publishing
LifeWay Church Resources
One LifeWay Plaza
Nashville, Tennessee 37234-0172

We believe that the Bible has God for its author; salvation for its end; and truth, without any mixture of error, for its matter and that all Scripture is totally true and trustworthy. The 2000 statement of The Baptist Faith and Message is our doctrinal guideline.

All Scripture quotations are taken from the Holman Christian Standard Bible®, copyright © 1999, 2000, 2002, 2003 by Holman Bible Publishers. Used by permission.

A Note from the Super Duper Editorial Team ...

Do you ever start studying your Sunday School or Wednesday night Bible study curriculum and think, *This is never going to work for my kids*?

Maybe you know you should be teaching your preschoolers biblical truths at home but don't know how. Perhaps you've been looking for something to fill downtime during Mother's Day Out. If you've ever found yourself in one of these situations, you are going to love this book. This book is packed full of *SUPER DUPER* age-appropriate, *FUN and EXCITING* biblically sound, *ABSOLUTELY* varied Bible activities that are sure to provide hours of *THOUGHT-IGNITING* fun.

From its conception, this book has been designed to provide practical, fun, and understandable activities you can use with one preschooler or twenty! Based upon the Levels of Biblical Learning™ concept areas, each chapter of this book helps you build a firm, biblical foundation for each child in your care. You'll find lots of crafts, games, and other activities for each area: *God, Jesus, Bible, Church, Creation, Self, Family,* and *Community and World.* There's even a chapter full of holiday activities! Plus, this book includes helpful articles to benefit your teaching, as well as a CD-ROM full of excellent teaching helps!

It is our prayer that this book will become a staple resource in your biblical teaching of children. A child's spiritual foundation is the most important foundation that can ever be built.

Jeff Land—*Compilation and Editing*
Alyssa Reeves—*Assembly and Editing*
Trudy Gardner—*Editing*

LifeWay Kids Promise

At LifeWay, we work hard to know kids. We take time to understand how they play and how they learn. And we know you need resources you can count on to connect kids to God's Word—leading them toward knowing Christ and growing in relationship with Him. That's why LifeWay Kids promises to offer foundational resources that are biblically sound, age appropriate, fun, and easy to use. These foundational resources help kids hear God's Word, know God's Word, and do God's Word by learning to apply it to their lives.

HEAR · KNOW · DO

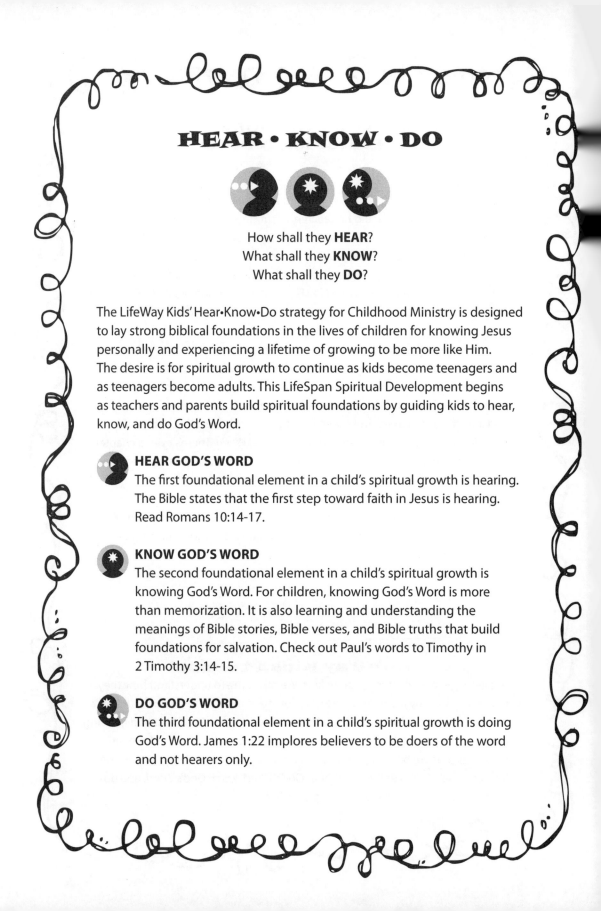

How shall they **HEAR**?
What shall they **KNOW**?
What shall they **DO**?

The LifeWay Kids' Hear·Know·Do strategy for Childhood Ministry is designed to lay strong biblical foundations in the lives of children for knowing Jesus personally and experiencing a lifetime of growing to be more like Him. The desire is for spiritual growth to continue as kids become teenagers and as teenagers become adults. This LifeSpan Spiritual Development begins as teachers and parents build spiritual foundations by guiding kids to hear, know, and do God's Word.

HEAR GOD'S WORD
The first foundational element in a child's spiritual growth is hearing. The Bible states that the first step toward faith in Jesus is hearing. Read Romans 10:14-17.

KNOW GOD'S WORD
The second foundational element in a child's spiritual growth is knowing God's Word. For children, knowing God's Word is more than memorization. It is also learning and understanding the meanings of Bible stories, Bible verses, and Bible truths that build foundations for salvation. Check out Paul's words to Timothy in 2 Timothy 3:14-15.

DO GOD'S WORD
The third foundational element in a child's spiritual growth is doing God's Word. James 1:22 implores believers to be doers of the word and not hearers only.

Contents

Absolutely Iconic

Activities are categorized by a series of icons. For your convenience, each icon is explained below. Activities are scaled 1-3 based on age appropriateness:

Babies through 2s   *3s through Pre-K*   *Kindergarten*

Each activity is categorized by learning area. There are 7 activity types in this book.

 Art activities encourage preschoolers to draw, paint, or create scenes from a Bible story.

 Homeliving activities help preschoolers apply the activity to their daily lives.

 Blocks activities encourage preschoolers to build and create as a result of what they are learning.

 Puzzles and manipulatives activities help preschoolers use their hands and develop fine motor skills while learning.

 Dramatic play activities encourage preschoolers to participate in role plays to reinforce learning.

 Science and nature activities guide preschoolers to explore God's amazing creation as a method of learning.

 Music and books activities help verbal and auditory learners understand biblical concepts.

Levels of Biblical Learning™

Each activity is assigned one of the eight Levels of Biblical Learning™ (LOBL) concept areas to help guide kids on their spiritual growth journey. A copy of the LOBL, as well as a complete explanation of each level, is found on the CD-ROM in the back of this book.

Super Duper: How To

This book is filled with wonderful activities for teaching preschoolers about God and His wonderful creation. To better understand each page, a practical explanation is provided on **page 136**. Each activity is based upon one of the Levels of Biblical Learning™ concept areas. You can use this book in a variety of ways. Here are some ideas for using this book at home, at church, and beyond!

Home Use: Teaching your child about God is one of the greatest privileges you have as a parent; however, it might be difficult to think of creative ways to teach your child about the truth of God's love. The idea of being your child's spiritual leader might be a little scary! It is, nonetheless, your command from God.

> *Love the LORD your God with all your heart, with all your soul, and with all your strength. These words that I am giving you today are to be in your heart. Repeat them to your children. Talk about them when you sit in your house and when you walk along the road, when you lie down and when you get up. Bind them as a sign on your hand and let them be a symbol on your forehead. Write them on the doorposts of your house and on your gates.*
> **Deuteronomy 6:5-9**

Here are some ideas for using this book at home:
- Plan a daily activity. Use one activity from this book each day to teach an important biblical concept.
- Use games and crafts from this book once a week on a special family night.
- When keeping children in the home, make constructive use of the time you have with them by planning a craft activity.
- Read the articles for important tips on how you can assist your child in learning about God and His world.
- Tell your child the foundational Bible stories found on the CD-ROM.

Church Use: Preschoolers are constantly learning by seeing, doing, touching, smelling, and going. Every time a preschooler enters your church, be prepared to teach him about God's truth. Jesus believed in the importance of teaching children.

Jesus said, "Leave the children alone, and don't try to keep them from coming to Me, because the kingdom of heaven is made up of people like this."
Matthew 19:14

Here are some ideas for using this book at church:
- Replace a suggested activity in the curriculum. Choose an activity from the same suggested Levels of Biblical Learning™ concept area.
- Provide this resource for substitute teachers to use for planning sessions.
- Use for teaching preschoolers during a day camp or parents night out.
- Use anytime preschoolers are at church for special occasions such as holiday services, conferences, and so forth.
- Plan training sessions for your teaching staff with the plans provided on the CD-ROM which compliment the articles found within this book.

Other Uses: Learning can take place in any setting. Preschoolers learn from grandparents, teachers, parents, and many others. God gave humanity a huge classroom and preschoolers are constantly learning in a variety of environments.

They will all be taught by God. Everyone who has listened to and learned from the Father comes to Me.
John 6:45

Here are some other ideas for using this book:
- Use the activities in this book for private school or homeschool lesson plans.
- Use for "cousins camp" when preschoolers are visiting grandparents.
- Give as a gift to parents at baby dedications.
- Share with other parents of preschoolers, especially those who may not have grown up in Christian homes and may not understand their roles as their children's spiritual leaders.

CHAPTER 1
God

About the LOBL Concept Area: God

A professor I had in seminary used this phrase: "God created the child with the capacity to learn about Him." That phrase has been a major influence in my thoughts about teaching children. I believe it is important to begin talking to children about God in infancy and throughout their lives.

As adults, we have an opportunity to build a child's understanding about God and how she can relate to Him. I was recently telling my kindergarten Sunday School class the story of Ezra reading the Bible scroll to the men and women of Israel. They were surprised at how long Ezra actually read the Bible (from morning until noon). We talked about how the people worshiped God and celebrated with each other. I am amazed at how much the children understood about singing and worshiping God.

On another occasion a child asked, "Does God hear me when I think?" I was surprised at her level of thinking. She then remarked, "What if I am not thinking anything?" Again, I must remember the child has limited knowledge, but she is trying to put it all together in her mind. I responded, "He knows all of what you are thinking."

Children begin to build an understanding about God from how teachers and parents talk about God. Teachers of babies–2s use their voices to say, "God loves you." Teachers of 3s–pre-k say, "God loves all people." Teachers of kindergartners say, "God shows His love to all people." Our voices, songs, pictures, and use of the Bible continue to build many concepts about God's love, care, and provision for all people. Through preparation (reading and studying the biblical content) teachers engage the child to help her hear about God, know who God is, and ultimately to do what He says.

Ann Edwards

Important Note About Allergies:

When working with preschoolers it is important to always be aware of allergies. When using this book in a classroom setting, please print the allergy alert from the CD-ROM and inform parents of ingredients or nature items used in the activity.

SCIENCE
& Nature

Storm in a Jar

Guide kids to tear foil into tiny pieces and roll them into balls. Follow the CD-ROM directions to make storm jars. Add the foil balls and two drops of liquid soap to each jar of water. Be sure the lid is sealed tightly; then show kids how to twirl the jar to make a "storm."
- Tell the Bible story "Elijah Prayed for Rain" (1 Kings 18:1-2,41-46) as kids work.
- Share that the Bible teaches people to pray and ask God for help. God hears people when they pray.

- aluminum foil
- clear plastic jars with lids
- glue
- liquid soap
- water
- blue food color
- "Create a Storm Jar" (CD-ROM)

CHANGE IT UP!

Creation

- God Made the World (Genesis 1:1–2:3)
- God gave the rain to help water plants and make things grow. God gives people everything you need.

FAMILY

- Noah and the Ark (Genesis 6–9)
- God protected Noah's family from the flood. God loves families and helps each family member.

Self

- Daniel Chose Good Food (Daniel 1:1-20)
- Rain helps plants to grow. Fruits and vegetables are good for kids' bodies.

• soft-sided cars

Rolling, Rolling, Rolling

• Put several cars on the floor for babies to push and roll.
• As babies play, tell them their families ride in cars to church to learn about God. Mention that people in the Bible walked to the places they needed to go.
• Talk to baby: "God told people He loved them. God loves you and cares for you."

CHANGE IT UP!

Talk to baby: "You ride in the car with your family. Your family is special to God."

Talk to baby: "People ride to church in cars. God wants you to come to church. Church is a special place."

Talk to baby: "People ride in cars to go different places. God made the world."

A Maze of Blocks

- wooden blocks
- sand—Place in a shallow container.
- blue paper squares

- Invite kids to make a maze in the sand using blocks.
- Tell kids the Bible story "The Israelites Crossed the Red Sea" (Exodus 14:15-31). Suggest that kids make a maze from Egypt to the Red Sea or a maze across the Red Sea. Encourage them to use blue paper as water.
- Remind kids that only God could move the waters of the Red Sea so that the people could cross on dry land.

- Jesus Calmed the Storm (Mark 4:1-2,35-41)
- God gave Jesus the power to stop the storm. Jesus is God's Son.

- Noah and the Ark (Genesis 6–9)
- God protected Noah's family from the flood. God loves families and helps each family member.

- The People Crossed the Jordan River (Joshua 3–4)
- God gave the Israelites a way to cross the Jordan River. God loves and cares for all people.

- construction paper
- glue sticks

Make a Tear Art Collage

- Direct kids to use one sheet of construction paper as the background for their pictures.
- Demonstrate how to tear other pieces of construction paper to make mountains, streams, sky, clouds, trees, and other things they might see in the mountains.
- Show kids how to use glue to attach the torn pieces to their papers to make pictures.
- Tell kids the Bible story "Elijah Prayed for Rain" (1 Kings 18:1-2,41-46) as they work.
- Share that God can do anything.

CHANGE IT UP!

- Timothy Learned About God (Acts 16:1-3; 2 Timothy 1:1-5; 3:14-17)
- Make a Bible collage. Share that God gave the Bible so people can know about Him.

- God Made the World (Genesis 1:1–2:3)
- Make a creation collage. Share that God made the world and everything in it. He made the light, dark, stars, sun, plants, animals, and people.

- Joseph Helped His Brothers (Genesis 45:1-11,16-28; 46:28-34; 47:1-11)
- Make a family collage. Share that Joseph loved his brothers. God wants kids to love their brothers and sisters.

Make "Raindrop" Art

- Add a different food color to each cup of water. Show kids how to fill an eyedropper with colored water and drip it onto a coffee filter to make a design.
- Compare the drops of water to raindrops.
- Tell the Bible story "Noah" (Genesis 6–9).
- Mention that God loves and cares for each person and shows His love in many ways.

- eyedroppers
- plastic cups of water
- food color
- white coffee filters
- waterproof smocks

 CHANGE IT UP!

- Elijah Prayed for Rain (1 Kings 18:1-2,41-46)
- God has power over everything, including the weather.

- Jesus Talked to the Woman at the Well (John 4:6-11,19-30,39-42)
- Jesus told the woman about God's love. Jesus wants kids to tell people about God's love.

- God Made the World (Genesis 1:1–2:3)
- God made the world and everything in it. Kids can thank God for what He made.

DRAMATIC PLAY

- brown paper sacks
- scissors
- glue or tape
- yarn
- construction paper
- crayons

Create a Centurion Uniform

- Cut head and arm holes in each sack. Cut slits along the bottom of the bags to make large fringe.
- Encourage kids to cut out paper designs to glue to the uniforms.
- Allow kids to color buttons, medals, and stripes on their uniforms.
- Help kids tie yarn around their waists as sashes.
- Tell the Bible story "Peter Visited Cornelius" (Acts 10:1-33).
- Share that God cares for people. He shows His care for them in many ways.

CHANGE IT UP!

- Jesus Is Alive (John 20:1-18)
- God raised Jesus from the dead. Kids can know that Jesus is alive.
- Remind kids that there were guards at Jesus' tomb.

- Paul and Silas in Prison (Acts 16:22-32,34)
- Paul and Silas were able to tell the prison guard about God using Scripture from the Bible.

- David and Goliath (1 Samuel 17)
- David was a brave young man. Kids can be brave because God will help them not be afraid.

SCIENCE
&
Nature

Measure Distance

Encourage kids to look at the maps. Point out your town or state on the maps.

Allow kids to measure distance between places on the map. Tell the Bible story "Peter Visited Cornelius" (Acts 10:1-33). Note that the distance between Peter's house and Cornelius's house was 30 miles.

- Remind kids that God loves them wherever they are.

- city and state maps
- atlas
- Bible atlas
- rulers

CHANGE IT UP!

- Jesus Was Born (Luke 2:1-20)
- God sent Jesus to earth because He loves people. God wants kids to love Jesus.
- Talk about how far Mary and Joseph had to travel.

- Philip and the Ethiopian (Acts 8:26-39)
- Philip helped the Ethiopian learn about God using the Bible scroll. God wants kids to learn about Him by reading the Bible.
- Help kids think about the distance that the Ethiopian traveled in his chariot.

- God Gave Rules to the People (Exodus 19:1–20:21)
- God knew that people needed rules. Rules help people know what to do.
- Remind the kids that the people wandered in the desert for a long time.

SCIENCE
&
Nature

- coffee filters, water, cups, food color
- scissors, construction paper, glue, markers
- Add a different food color to each cup of water.

Create Coffee Filter Flowers and Birds

- Help kids fold or cut their coffee filters into smaller pieces.
- Assist kids in dipping their folded or cut filters into the cups of colored water. Squeeze the excess water out of the filters.
- Allow kids to glue their damp, dyed filters to construction paper to create flowers and birds.
- Encourage kids to use markers to embellish their pictures.
- As kids work, tell the Bible story "God Made the World" (Genesis 1:1–2:3). Remind kids that God cares for the birds and the flowers. God cares for everyone.

CHANGE IT UP!

JESUS

- Children Sang for Jesus (Matthew 21:1-11,14-16)
- Children worshiped Jesus as He arrived in town. Jesus deserves kids' worship.

Creation

- Noah (Genesis 6–9)
- God loves and cares for each person and shows His love in many ways.

Self

- Jesus Taught About Worry (Matthew 6:26-29)
- God will take care of each person. He hears and answers prayers.

Make Flat Bread

Tell the Bible story "Elijah and the Widow" (1 Kings 17:10-16). Guide kids to mix dry ingredients together and wet ingredients together in separate bowls. Allow them to pour the wet ingredients into the dry ingredients and stir until smooth.
Explain that in Bible times, bread cooked flat. People used oil and flour to make bread.

- Add oil to skillet, pour two tablespoons batter onto skillet, and cook bread (like pancakes). Place cooked bread on paper towels to drain excess oil.
- Guide kids to understand the difference between needs and wants. (Needs are the things people must have to live; wants are things people would like to have.)
- Remind kids that God will provide for all of their needs.

CHANGE IT UP!

- Jesus Fed the People (John 6:1-13)
- Jesus showed His love for people by helping them.

- The Good Samaritan (Luke 10:25-37)
- The Samaritan cared about the needs of the injured man. God wants kids to show love and care for all people.

- Ruth and Boaz (Ruth 1:22; 2:1-23)
- Boaz helped meet Ruth's need for food. God wants kids to help people in need.

- ½ cup whole wheat flour, ⅓ cup self-rising flour, 1 tablespoon brown sugar, 2 eggs, 2 cups buttermilk, 1 tablespoon oil
- electric skillet
- paper towels
- mixing bowls
- measuring cups
- measuring and mixing spoons
- metal or rubber spatula

DRAMATIC PLAY

Play "Sticks" Games

- rhythm sticks (or ½-inch dowel rods— Cut into 12-inch lengths and smooth cut ends with sandpaper.)

- Guide kids to stand facing the leader.
- Call out various commands such as *touch your nose*, *stretch your hands high in the air*, and *hop in place*.
- Instruct kids to stand still like a stick when you call "Sticks!" Kids may stand straight with arms by side, or with arms sticking out like branches.
- Distribute rhythm sticks. Guide kids to balance their sticks on the backs of their hands, on their heads, on their knees, on their feet, and so forth.
- Help them distinguish between left and right by calling commands of which hand to hold the stick. Kids may also pass their sticks to others.
- Remind kids of the Bible story "Elijah and the Widow" (1 Kings 17:10-16).
- Help kids understand that God provides for every need. The widow needed oil and flour for bread, but she also needed sticks for the fire to cook the bread.

CHANGE IT UP!

JESUS

- Jesus Loved Zacchaeus (Luke 19:1-10)
- Showing love and kindness to everyone is important because Jesus loves all people.

Creation

- God Made Everything (Genesis 1:1–2:3)
- God made the earth and everything in it. He made the plants, trees, and flowers.

CHURCH

- Solomon Built the Temple (1 Kings 6)
- Lead kids to talk about materials people use when building, like wood from trees.

Super Duper Bible Skills for Preschoolers

One of the most precious gifts you can give your preschooler is her own Bible. At a young age preschoolers can begin to recognize the importance and value of God's special book. Select a Bible your preschooler can use for many years. Using the same Bible reinforces repetition, one of the best ways for preschoolers to learn. As your preschooler sees the same pictures, hears the same stories, and begins to read the same words, she can understand that the Bible is a valuable book for her life.

CHOOSE IT

- *Size*—The Bible should be large enough to hold easily, but not too large or too heavy to carry. The words should be large enough to read.
- *Complete*—Preschoolers need to know that both Testaments are included in the Bible and are equally important. Choose a complete Bible rather than Bible storybooks.
- *User friendly*—Consider purchasing a Bible that contains a table of contents and study helps.
- *Realistic illustrations*—Pictures in the Bible should be as realistic as possible. Avoid cartoon illustrations that may confuse your preschooler's understanding that the people and stories in the Bible are true.
- *Translation*—Choose an accurate translation of the biblical text rather than a paraphrase. The best Bible translations for children combine reliability with readability.
- *Durability*—Make sure the cover is of good quality. Consider purchasing a Bible carrying case that will protect and add length to the life of a child's Bible. Allow your preschooler to help choose her own cover.

USE IT

- *Interact and learn*—Allow your preschooler to:
  - carry her Bible
  - take it to Sunday School and worship services
  - turn the pages
  - explore its contents
- *Build and learn*—Offer play dough to your child and ask her to build the item found in each of the following verses:

- Exodus 31:18 (two stone tablets)
- Deuteronomy 17:18 (scroll)
- 2 Kings 4:10 (room with bed, table, chair, lamp)
- 1 Samuel 16:1,12-13 (horn of oil)
- Numbers 13:23 (bunch of grapes)
- *Hear and learn*—Ask your preschooler to make the sound found in each of the following verses:
  - Exodus 19:19 (trumpet)
  - 1 Chronicles 15:19 (cymbals)
  - 1 Kings 18:45 (rain)
  - John 20:13 (crying)
  - Mark 4:37 (wind)

Each interaction with the Bible prepares the way for spiritual conversion and transformation in your preschooler's life. A Bible—now is the time to choose it and use it.

Kelli McAnally

Looking for a Bible for your preschooler?
Try the **Read to Me Bible for Kids.**
HCSB® (ISBN-13: 9781586401726)
KJV (ISBN-13: 9781558198456)

CHAPTER 2
Jesus

About the LOBL Concept Area: Jesus

We had been looking at pictures of Jesus and hearing His name as cheerful music played in the background. We had turned pages in the Bible to find pictures of Jesus. We had talked about Jesus and His love. It had been a morning filled with proclamations of Jesus' name. I noticed Emma walk to a large piece of sticky plastic fastened to the wall. Several picture cutouts were spread around for Emma and her friends to choose. Picking up a picture from the pile, Emma, just 20 months old, said "Jesus" as she stuck the picture on the plastic.

My heart swelled with confirmation that what I do every week with Emma and her preschool friends does make a difference. Even though Emma may not understand all the words I say or relate to every story or activity in a personal way, she can hear the name of our Savior and repeat His name. Emma can know that Jesus loves her and cares about her. Emma can know she is included in the ones Jesus invited into His presence when He said, "Let the little children come to Me" (Mark 10:14).

Don't think that what you do does not matter. On the contrary, everything you do in Jesus' name does matter—now and for eternity.

Rachel Coe

Important Note About Allergies:

When working with preschoolers it is important to always be aware of allergies. When using this book in a classroom setting, please print the allergy alert from the CD-ROM and inform parents of ingredients or nature items used in the activity.

Explore Rocks

Allow kids to sort, measure, and wash rocks using the materials provided.
Talk about kinds and uses of rocks.
Share the Bible story "Jesus Is Alive" (John 20:1-18).
Point out that the rock used to cover the place where Jesus' body was placed was likely a huge, round boulder.

 CHANGE IT UP!

- The Ten Commandments (Exodus 19:1–20:21)
- God loves people even when they disobey.

- God Created the World (Genesis 1:1–2:3)
- God created the earth and everything in it.

- David and Goliath (1 Samuel 17)
- People can trust God to take care of their needs and safety.

- rocks
- toothbrushes
- rulers
- spray bottles— Fill with water.

JESUS

- PVC pipe
- connectors to match the size of pipe

Talk Through PVC Pipes and Connectors

- Cut the pipe into various lengths. Choose different kinds of connectors that fit the pipe.
- Show kids how to fit the pipes and connectors together.
- Encourage them to whisper something about Jesus to each other through their pipe creations.
- Remind kids that when Jesus was on earth, people gathered water from wells, unlike today when pipes bring people water.
- Tell the Bible story "Jesus Talked with the Woman at the Well" (John 4:6-11,19-30,39-42) while kids work.

CHANGE IT UP!

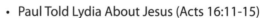

- Nehemiah Prayed (Nehemiah 1:1-4; 2:1-8,17-18; 3)
- People show they love God by obeying Him.

- Paul Told Lydia About Jesus (Acts 16:11-15)
- God wants people to tell others about Him.

- Paul and Barnabas Told About Jesus (Acts 13:1-5,13-16,32-33,42-51)
- Missionaries tell people about God and Jesus.

earch and Find

Bury the items in the sand.
Guide kids to use their hands to dig in the sand and find items that remind them of ways to help.
Share the Bible story "Jesus Chose Special Helpers" (Matthew 4:18-22; 10:1-4) while they work.
Encourage kids to help Jesus by following His example.

- sand—Place in a shallow container.
- helping items (spray bottle, dog toy, baby rattle, toy car, and so forth)

CHANGE IT UP!

- God Created Man and Woman (Genesis 2:7–3:23)
- God gave people the ability to make choices.
- Hide creation items such as flowers, toy animals, and so forth.

- David Praised and Thanked God (1 Chronicles 15:1-4,11-12,14-28)
- God wants people to praise and thank Him.
- Hide items for which people thank God, such as photos of friends, toy houses, and so forth.

- A Church Helped (Acts 11:19-30)
- God wants people to help at church.
- Hide pictures of items that people use to help, such as a broom, washcloth, and so forth.

JESUS

* play dough
* shoes with different soles
* foot-shaped cookie cutters

Make Prints in Play Dough

* Lead preschoolers to press the shoes and foot shapes into play dough.
* Share the Bible story "Jesus Chose Special Helpers" (Matthew 4:18-22; 10:1-4) while they work.
* Explain that Jesus asked some men to follow Him and help Him tell about God. Everyone can help Jesus by telling about God.

CHANGE IT UP!

* God Cared for Noah (Genesis 6–9)
* God cares and provides for people.
* Use people-shaped cookie cutters.

* Miriam Loved Her Family (Exodus 2:1-10)
* People can show love for their families.
* Use people-shaped cookie cutters.

* A Woman Gave an Offering (Mark 12:41-44)
* At church people give offerings.
* Press coins into the play dough.

1 2 3

Watch Water Travel

SCIENCE & Nature

- ink pens
- paper towels
- plastic bowls

Pour 2 inches of water into each plastic bowl.
Invite kids to use the ink pens to scribble, draw a picture, or write their names in the middle of a paper towel.
Place the top 3 inches of the paper towel directly in the bowl of water. Drape the remaining paper towel over the edge of the bowl.
Watch as the water travels up the paper towel and onto the ink. Allow several minutes for the water to move completely through the paper towel.
While the water travels, tell kids the Bible story "Zacchaeus Met Jesus" (Luke 19:1-10).
Remind kids that while traveling, Jesus took the time to talk to Zacchaeus and be his friend. Jesus wants everyone to be His friend.

CHANGE IT UP!

- The People Crossed the Jordan River (Joshua 3–4)
- God shows His love to all people.

- God Created the World (Genesis 1:1–2:3)
- God created the earth and everything in it.

- Abram Moved to a New Home (Genesis 12:1-9)
- People show love for God when they obey Him.

DRAMATIC PLAY

- swim noodle
- 2 large plastic funnels
- clear packaging tape

Talk Through a Noodle Phone

- Lead kids to build a noodle phone by placing the narrow end of a funnel into each end of the swim noodle. Secure the funnels with tape.
- Invite kids to take turns listening and talking to a friend through the noodle phone.
- Share the Bible story "Jesus Fed the People" (John 6:1-13) as they work.
- Remind kids that Jesus told many people about God, but He never used a noodle phone! Encourage kids to think of people they can tell about God.

CHANGE IT UP!

- Josiah Read the Lost Bible Scroll (2 Kings 22:1-13; 23:1-3)
- The stories in the Bible are true.

- Paul Told Lydia About Jesus (Acts 16:11-15)
- People should tell their friends about Jesus.

- Andrew Told His Brother About Jesus (John 1:35-42)
- Missionaries tell people about God and Jesus.

1 | 2 | 3

JESUS

ook Layered Biscuits

Preheat the electric skillet to 300 degrees.

Separate the layers of each biscuit to make flat pieces.

Place the pieces in the skillet. Cook the layers like pancakes.

Tell kids about "Jesus' Special Supper" (Matthew 26:17-30) while the biscuits cook.

Place a small dab of butter on each biscuit once cooked.

Invite kids to sprinkle the cinnamon and sugar mixture on their biscuits.

Remind kids that Jesus told His disciples to remember Him when they ate this special supper. Kids can remember Jesus when they eat their biscuits.

- electric skillet
- spatula
- canned layered biscuits
- butter
- cinnamon and sugar mixture

CHANGE IT UP!

- God Helped the People Leave Egypt (Exodus 12–16)
- God is real. God can do all things. God provided food for the Israelites.

- Ruth Took Care of Her Family (Ruth 1:22; 2:1-23)
- Family members love one another.

- Jesus Showed Love to Zacchaeus (Luke 19:1-10)
- Jesus cares for all people.

Make Story Cloths

- muslin fabric
- markers
- scissors
- yardstick

- Cut a 20-inch square of muslin fabric for each child.
- Draw lines on the fabric, outlining four 10-by-10-inch squares.
- Distribute fabric and markers.
- Guide kids to draw pictures associated with Jesus. Share several of your favorite stories about Jesus.
- Invite kids to use their story cloths to tell their friends about Jesus.

CHANGE IT UP!

- God Cared for Elijah (1 Kings 17:1-6)
- Illustrate the story using the directions above.
- God can do all things.

- Philip Explained the Bible (Acts 8:26-39)
- Illustrate the story using the directions above.
- The Bible tells what God and Jesus are like.

CHURCH

- The People Read the Bible (Acts 17:1-4,10-12)
- Illustrate the story using the directions above.
- People at church worship, pray, give, sing, read the Bible, and listen to teaching and preaching.

Make Paper Chains

Show kids the disciples' names in Matthew 4:18-22; 10:1-4.
Practice pronouncing each disciple's name with the kids.
Distribute "Disciples" and scissors. Direct kids to cut apart the names.
Encourage kids to decorate the strips.
Model how to coil and tape the paper strips together, interlinking each strip.
Help kids remember that they can be like the disciples and help others know about Jesus.

CHANGE IT UP!

- God Took Care of the Animals (Genesis 6–9)
- Write the names of animals on the strips and complete activity as described.
- God provides for His creation.

- Jonathan Loved His Friend (1 Samuel 14:49; 18:1-4; 20)
- Write the names of friends on the strips and complete activity as described.
- People's choices can make them happy or sad.

- Jesus' Family Went to Church (Luke 2:22-40)
- Write the names of family members on the strips and complete activity as described.
- People at church worship, pray, give, sing, read the Bible, and listen to teaching and preaching.

- scissors
- tape
- construction paper
- crayons or markers
- embellishments (sequins, beads, stickers, ribbon)
- "Disciples" (CD-ROM)—Print and copy onto different colors of construction paper.

CHURCH

JESUS

DRAMATIC PLAY

- 6 chairs
- clipboards
- pencils

Play "Ambulance Rescue"

- Arrange the chairs to resemble an ambulance: push four chairs together to make a place for a child to lie down and add two chairs in front for driver/passenger seats.
- Model how kids can use the chairs as an ambulance to "drive" their friends to the hospital.
- Distribute clipboards and pencils.
- Demonstrate how to record the symptoms of the "injured" classmates.
- Allow kids to play "Ambulance Rescue" as time allows.
- Tell kids the Bible story "Four Friends Who Helped" (Mark 2:1-12).
- Remind kids that they can help their friends and family members by praying for them.

CHANGE IT UP!

Self

- The Good Samaritan (Luke 10:25-37)
- People can make right choices.

CHURCH

- The Church Chose Helpers (Acts 6:1-7)
- The church provides ways for people to help others.

COMMUNITY & WORLD

- People Prayed for Peter (Acts 12:1-17)
- People can be a part of God's work.

Thought-Igniting Words
Preschoolers Understand

Adults confuse preschoolers. Often the words and phrases they use have odd or strange meanings to a 3- or 4-year-old. Preschoolers think in very concrete terms and have few life experiences. Preschoolers interpret what they hear in basic, literal ways; adults often use symbolic and abstract language. This combination can lead to confusion and misunderstanding.

One of my favorite children's books is *The King Who Rained* by Fred Gwynne. This book illustrates a child's literal understanding. The king is illustrated hanging in the sky with torrents of rain falling from him. Children have difficulty with words that are homonyms (words that have double meanings), homophones (words that sound the same), or symbolic phrases.

When talking about biblical and spiritual issues, adults often use symbolic language. Think about these phrases and the pictures they may create in the mind of a concrete thinker:

- God's house
- Lamb of God
- Asking Jesus to live in your heart
- Body of Christ
- Standing on God's Word

As you talk with your child, use words and phrases that mean exactly what you want to say. Use *church* and *Bible* rather than *God's house* and *God's book*.

Remember that your child is beginning to learn about God and His love for her. She is just beginning to discover who Jesus is and the things He did. As you tell Bible stories and talk about Bible concepts, keep your conversations based on basic, foundational truths. Encourage your child to ask questions and think about what she knows. Answer questions simply and briefly. Allow your child to ask for more information.

Help your child develop strong, true, clear understandings about the Bible, God, and Jesus. As she grows, she will understand those more abstract ideas because she has a concrete foundation.

R. Scott Wiley

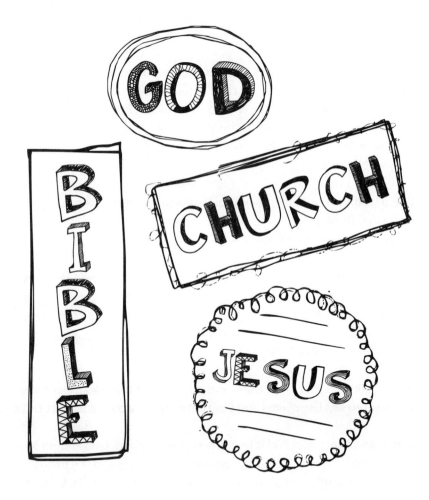

BIBLE

About the LOBL Concept Area: Bible

Sitting on the floor in a Sunday School class, I watch Cal toddle across the room. He stops by the Bible on the floor, picks it up, and carries it clutched to his chest. He approaches and drops the Bible in my lap. Each week Cal repeats this ritual with me. Today something different happens.

> "Bible," Cal says. He has never said this before.
> "Yes," I say. "You found the Bible."
> As always, Cal sits beside me and begins to turn pages.
> He pauses at a picture.
> "Jesus," Cal says. This too is new.
> "Jesus," I repeat. "The Bible tells us about Jesus."

Our weekly ritual has helped Cal have a personal experience with the Bible. He has learned that the Bible is a book, a special book about God and Jesus. He has learned that the Bible is a book for him. He has connected his life with the truths of the Bible.

How can you help a child develop concepts about the Bible? Provide a Bible for a child to handle, carry, and use. Teach a child to handle the Bible carefully, but don't get too upset if pages are torn accidently. Tape the pages and thank God that kids can learn firsthand about the Bible. Use paper strips to mark Bible verses or stories. Guide a child to open the Bible to the marked page. Say the verse or talk about the Bible story. Point to a key word or name.

Developing concepts about the Bible is essential to learning spiritual truths. The Bible contains what God wants us to know about Him. A child who hears and begins to know and do what the Bible says will have a strong foundation for spiritual growth.

R. Scott Wiley

Important Note About Allergies:

When working with preschoolers it is important to always be aware of allergies. When using this book in a classroom setting, please print the allergy alert from the CD-ROM and inform parents of ingredients or nature items used in the activity.

Written in Sand

Guide each child to write the words *Jesus* and *Bible* on his paper. Allow him to gently trace over the letters with a line of glue. Instruct him to hold his paper over the container of sand and sprinkle sand over the glue.

- Allow kids to use markers to decorate their papers.

- construction paper
- markers
- glue
- shallow container of sand

CHANGE IT UP!

- Jesus and the Woman at the Well (John 4:6-11,19-30,39-42)
- Guide kids to write the words *Jesus* and *God*.
- Jesus taught people what God is like.

- God Created the World (Genesis 1:1–2:3)
- Guide kids to write the words *God* and *Create*.
- God created the earth and everything in it.

- Abram Moved to a New Home (Genesis 12:1-9)
- Guide kids to write the words *Obey* and *God*.
- People show love for God by obeying Him.

BIBLE

Shaving Cream Spell Off

- index cards
- marker
- non-menthol shaving cream or baby lotion

- Write the words *Bible* and *words* on index cards.
- Show kids the word cards. Tell them that Baruch wrote down the words from God. Tell the Bible story "Jeremiah and Baruch" (Jeremiah 36:1-4).
- Provide a handful of shaving cream for each child. Show her how to smooth it on the table. Guide her to use her fingers to print letters in the shaving cream such as *B,I,B,L,E* and *W,O,R,D,S*. Children may want to print other letters they know. If completing this activity with younger children, encourage them to draw pictures of the Bible in their shaving cream.

CHANGE IT UP!

- Jesus Was Born (Luke 2:1-20)
- God sent Jesus to earth because He loves people.

- Adam and Eve's Choice (Genesis 2:7–3:23)
- God gave people the ability to make right choices.

- Jacob and Esau (Genesis 25:19-34; 27:1-45)
- People can recognize when they hurt others.

BIBLE

Magnet Mania

Write the words *Bible* and *help* on index cards.

Place magnetic letters in a bag and shake up the bag. Show kids the word cards.

Invite a child to find letters from the bag to spell the word *help* and to place the letters on the cookie sheet. Help her read the word.

Encourage her to find letters to spell and read the word *Bible*.

Children may enjoy spelling and reading other words made with the magnetic letters. As they work, tell them that Paul wrote a letter to Philemon. He wrote words that were made up of letters.

CHANGE IT UP!

- Cornelius Learned About God's Love (Acts 10:1-33)
- God shows His love to all people.
- Spell the word *love* and follow the directions above.

- Jesus and Bartimaeus (Mark 10:46-52)
- Jesus performed miracles and healed the sick.
- Spell the word *heal* and follow the directions above.

- Jonathan Loved His Friend (1 Samuel 14:49; 18:1-4; 20)
- People's choices can make them happy or sad.
- Spell the words *happy* and *sad* and follow the directions above.

- cookie sheet
- magnetic letters
- index cards

BIBLE

DRAMATIC PLAY

- Bible
- small tote bag

Bible in a Bag

- Encourage a child to place a Bible in a bag and carry it to a friend in the room.
- Talk about people you might see out the window who are carrying their Bibles.
- Share with the child that people at church read the Bible to learn about God.

SCIENCE & Nature

- child's step stool

Step It Up

- Invite a child to step up on the stool and step back down. Assist the child as needed.
- Tell the child that Ezra stood on a platform to read the Bible scroll.

HOME LIVING

- large crayons or washable markers
- newsprint

Newsprint Drawings

- Place the items on a low table. Invite kids to draw pictures of themselves. Share that Baruch wrote down God's words.
- Tell the Bible story "Jeremiah and Baruch" (Jeremiah 36:1-4). Point out that people read the Bible to learn about God. People learn from the Bible.

BIBLE

Going Fishing

Make a "boat" by removing the box flaps and trimming the sides to about waist high to preschoolers.

Tell kids that men used nets to catch fish in Bible times. Help a child climb in the "boat" and show her how to throw out the net. Another child can toss fish shapes onto the net, and then the first child can pull in the net. Children may swap places as they play. Tell the Bible story "Jesus Chose Special Helpers" (Matthew 4:18-22; 10:1-4). Like the fisherman, Jesus wants kids to tell others about God.

- large cardboard box
- fish net
- foam or paper fish shapes

CHANGE IT UP!

- The People Crossed the Jordan River (Joshua 3–4)
- God shows His love to all people.

- Jesus Fed the People (John 6:1-13)
- Jesus cares about each person's needs.

- Breakfast With Jesus (John 21:1-17)
- God wants people to care about their friends.

Gel Writing Tablets

- quart-sized ziplock bags
- colorless hair gel
- blue food color
- clear packing tape
- cotton swabs
- index cards—Write the following words on separate cards: *Jeremiah, Baruch, God, scroll, king, fire,* and *Bible* (older) or *draw Bible pictures* (younger).

- Tell the Bible story "Jeremiah and Baruch" (Jeremiah 36:1-4).
- Distribute ziplock bags.
- Guide kids to hold the bags open as you squeeze hair gel into them. Carefully drop 1 or 2 drops of food color into the hair gel.
- Seal the bags with clear packing tape.
- Encourage kids to squish the bags until the gel and food color mix together.
- Instruct boys and girls to use their writing tablets to write some Bible words.
- Distribute word cards and cotton swabs.
- Prompt kids to place the cards under their bags and trace over the letters or pictures with the cotton swabs.
- Comment that when people read the words Jeremiah and other people wrote in the Bible, they learn about God.

CHANGE IT UP!

- The Ten Commandments (Exodus 19:1–20:21)
- God wants people to obey Him.

- Jesus and the Woman at the Well (John 4:6-11,19-30,39-42)
- Jesus taught people what God is like.

- Ezra Read the Bible (Nehemiah 8:1-12)
- People at church learn from the Bible.

Hidden Messages

Tell the Bible story "Philip and the Ethiopian" (Acts 8:26-39). Point out that the man could see and read the words, but he could not understand them. Philip helped him understand.
- Give each child a piece of prepared copy paper.
- Invite kids to use the watercolor paints to paint their pages.
- Help kids read the hidden message. Remind kids that learning about Jesus made the Ethiopian man happy.

- copy paper
- watercolor paints
- paintbrushes
- white crayons—Write *Jesus said, "The Bible tells about Me."* (older) or draw a smiling face (younger) on copy paper. Make one for each child.

CHANGE IT UP!

- God Cared For Elijah (1 Kings 17:1-6)
- Write the message *God can do all things.*
- Follow the directions above to complete the activity.

- Jesus and Matthew's Friends (Matthew 9:9-13)
- Write the message *Jesus taught people what God is like.*
- Follow the directions above to complete the activity.

- A Church Chose Special Helpers (Acts 6:1-7)
- Write the message *Churches provide ways for people to help each other.*
- Follow the directions above to complete the activity.

Write Letters and Play Post Office

- paper and envelopes
- pens and pencils
- stickers
- cardboard box
- utility knife
  (teacher use)

- Place the box on its side on a table. Cut a narrow slit in the bottom of the box for preschoolers to insert envelopes for mailing.
- Arrange the paper and envelopes on another table. Help kids write notes or draw pictures to family members or friends.
- Guide them to deliver their mail to the "post office." Show them how to "stamp" the mail using a sticker.
- Mention that kids are writing words or drawing pictures they want people to know or see. Tell them that Baruch wrote words that God wants people to know. These words are found in
  the Bible.
- Open the Bible to the Book of Jeremiah. Tell the Bible story "Jeremiah and Baruch" (Jeremiah 36:1-4).

CHANGE IT UP!

- Paul Wrote God's Words in the Bible
  (Acts 17:1-4; 1 Thessalonians 3:2,6-8,11-13; 4)
- People wrote God's words in the Bible.

- The Angel Visited Mary (Luke 1:26-38)
- God sent a message to Mary about her baby through the angel.

- Timothy Learned About God
  (Acts 16:1-3; 2 Timothy 1:1-5; 3:14-17)
- God wants families to worship together.

Natural Writing Utensils

Pour tempera paint into a bowl and place it on the table with the paper.

- Invite kids to dip the tip of a nature item into the paint and use it to write on the vellum paper.
- As kids work, tell the Bible story "Jeremiah and Baruch" (Jeremiah 36:1-4). Point out that Baruch wrote the words Jeremiah said. Explain that Baruch probably used something similar to a pen made from a reed.
- Use the nature items to write *God gave us the Bible* on each child's paper. When the paint has dried, roll the ends of the vellum and tie it with string to make a scroll.

- liquid tempera paint
- small bowl
- vellum paper
- yarn or string
- various nature items (feathers, quills, twigs, seashells, rocks, and so forth)

BIBLE

CHANGE IT UP!

- God Gave Rules to Moses (Exodus 19:1–20:21)
- God wants people to obey Him.

- God Created the World (Genesis 1:1–2:3)
- God wants people to thank Him for His creation.

- The First Family (Genesis 1–4)
- God's plan for families is for mothers and fathers to raise children.
- Help kids write *God has a plan for my family.*

DRAMATIC PLAY

- cookie sheet
- large piece of fabric
- 10 items (clock, telephone, Bible, pencil, marker, and so forth)

BIBLE

30-Second Memory

- Display 10 items on a cookie sheet. Allow kids to look at the items for 30 seconds. Challenge them to remember what they see.
- Cover the tray with fabric and ask kids to recall the items.
- Vary the game by removing one item and allowing kids to guess what is missing.
- Ask kids if it was difficult to remember what was on the tray. Tell them that sometimes it is hard to remember things. God wants people to remember what the Bible says. At church people learn and remember what the Bible says.

₹ CHANGE IT UP!

JESUS

- Jesus Was Born (Luke 2:1-20)
- God sent Jesus to earth because He loves people.
- Place items associated with a baby on the cookie sheet and follow the directions above.

Self

- Abram Moved to a New Home (Genesis 12:1-9)
- People show love for God by obeying Him.
- Place items associated with a moving to a new house on the cookie sheet and follow the directions above.

CHURCH

- Jesus' Family Went to Church (Luke 2:22-40)
- People at church worship, pray, give, sing, read the Bible, and listen to teaching and preaching.
- Place items associated with church on the cookie sheet and follow the directions above.

The Super Duper
Mind-Body Learning Connection

In his book *Spark: The Revolutionary New Science of Exercise and the Brain*, Dr. John Ratey explores evidence that researchers have "nailed down a direct biological connection between movement and cognitive function."[1] Research has determined that there are pathways from the cerebellum (the part of the brain that coordinates motor movements) to parts of the brain involved in memory and attention.[2] These findings support the fact that when the body is engaged, the mind is engaged, and discipline problems decline.

Boys have higher levels of spinal fluid in the cerebellum, which makes their need for movement greater. In fact, messages between the brain and body move more quickly in boys when movement is involved.

FOUR REASONS TO INCORPORATE MOVEMENT

1. *Movement* activates most of the brain by increasing blood flow to the brain, enhancing alertness and attention.

2. *Movement* anchors new learning. Movement causes brain cells that fire together to bind together more readily, forming a new network of learning.

3. *Movement* influences memory. The brain forms memories based on the body's relationship to the surroundings. In other words, a child may remember that he was by the window when he repeated a fact about the Bible story.

4. *Movement* releases "happy hormones" that relax the body and get the mind ready to learn by increasing energy levels.

[1] John Ratey, *Spark: The Revolutionary New Science of Exercise and the Brain*, Little Brown and Company, 2008; p. 43.
[2] Eric Jensen, *Teaching with the Body in Mind*, Corwin Press, 2000; p. 22.

FIVE BRAIN ENERGIZERS THAT TEACH

1. *Body measures.* Ask kids to measure items around the room with their bodies and report the findings. For example, the manger is 8 hands long and 10 hands high. To add interest, ask kids to make a list of things to measure before beginning the activity.

2. *Color Hunt.* Ask kids to get up and touch five (or whatever number is suitable for your group) blue (any color) things around the room, and then return to their seats. Make this more fun by playing lively music and asking kids to return to their seats by the time the music stops.

3. *As If.* This activity can be used as an energizer or to teach or review Bible story concepts. Ask kids to …
   a. Run in place as if a big bear is chasing them.
   b. "Swim" as if they are in a giant pool of pudding.
   c. Shake their bodies as if they are wet dogs.
   d. "Climb" as if they are Zacchaeus climbing the tree to see Jesus.

4. *Learn a Bible verse.* Print the words to a Bible verse on 8½-by-11-inch pieces of paper (one word per sheet). Make several sets depending on the number of kids. Scatter the pieces of paper on the floor. Instruct kids to walk or march around the room until you call out a word in the verse. The kids then stand by a piece of paper with that word. Call out the words of the verse in order. To create a challenge, mix up the order.

5. *Stand and walk.* Instruct kids to walk quickly around the room when the music begins and to think of two ideas or facts they remember about the Bible story. When the music stops, ask kids to freeze. Then place kids in pairs and instruct them to share their two ideas with their partners. Placing kids in pairs allows every child an opportunity to participate and stay more focused on the activity.

Mary Ann Bradberry

CHAPTER 4
Creation

CREATION

About the LOBL Concept Area: Creation

"I want to see the monkeys!" squeals Esther.

"I want to see the hippos!" says Joy as she jumps up and down.

Going to the zoo with their parents and younger brother, Josiah, is always a lot of fun. As two-year-old twins of missionaries living in Lima, Peru, the girls have many opportunities to learn about God's creation. With the help of their parents, they learn that God made the animals, plants, sky, sun, moon, and stars. He made mommies, daddies, brothers, and sisters. God made everything!

It's always exciting to watch a child discover God's world! Young children are literal thinkers. From an early age, their understanding is based on what they see, hear, touch, smell, and taste. As a child hears a bird chirp, tastes a banana, or smells a daffodil, she learns that God wants her to enjoy the things He made. As she fills her dog's water bowl, the child learns that God wants people to take care of the things He made.

Rachel, the kids' mother, knows that one of the best ways to teach her children about God is by teaching them about His creation. As her children grow, she will teach them that God made people different from the other things He made, and He gave people the ability to make choices. She will show them how to care for the things God made, and she will teach them to be thankful to God—especially for His creation.

"Esther, what is this?" asks Mommy as she holds up a picture card.

"Cat," replies Esther.

"Joy, what sound does the cat make?" asks Mommy.

"Meow. Meow."

"And who made the kitty cat?"

"God," reply both girls.

"Yes, thank You, God, for cats," says Mommy.

"Thank You, God, for cats," echo the girls.

Debbie Ruth

Important Note About Allergies:

When working with preschoolers it is important to always be aware of allergies. When using this book in a classroom setting, please print the allergy alert from the CD-ROM and inform parents of ingredients or nature items used in the activity.

Race Water Dots

Tape a piece of waxed paper onto a cookie sheet.

Show kids how to use the eyedropper to squeeze water drops onto the waxed paper.

Guide kids to hold the cookie sheet and slowly tilt it back and forth. Encourage them to watch the water drops move across the waxed paper.

Place two drops at one edge of the waxed paper. Tilt the cookie sheet to allow the water drops to race down.

Remind kids that water was one of the first things God created. Tell the Bible story "God Made the World" (Genesis 1:1–2:3).

- cookie sheets
- waxed paper
- eyedropper
- cups of water
- tape

CREATION

CHANGE IT UP!

- The People Crossed the Jordan River (Joshua 3–4)
- God shows His love to all people.

- Jesus Calmed the Storm (Mark 4:1-2,35-41)
- Jesus performed miracles and healed the sick.

- Noah (Genesis 6–9)
- God wants people to obey Him.

SCIENCE
&
Nature

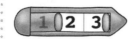

Sandstorm Creations

- plastic tablecloth
- masking tape
- funnel
- tub of sand
- twine or heavy string
- scoop or spoon
- broom, dustpan
- ice pick (teacher use)

- Spread a plastic tablecloth across the floor and tape down the edges.
- Use an ice pick to poke three evenly-spaced holes around the rim of a large funnel.
- Loop twine through the holes and gather the ends together so the funnel will hang evenly.
- Hang the funnel from the ceiling and position it several inches above the ground.
- Place a tub of sand, a scoop, a broom, and a dustpan on the tablecloth.
- Demonstrate how to scoop sand into the funnel and gently swing the twine to make designs on the tablecloth.
- Encourage kids to use the scoops to pour sand into the funnel. Allow them to make designs on the tablecloth by gently moving the funnel as the sand escapes. Sweep up the sand design and return sand to the tub before the next person's turn.
- Guide kids to take turns forming things God created.
- Share "God Made the World" (Genesis 1:1–2:3). Remind kids that God made the world and everything in it.

CHANGE IT UP!

- God Helped the People (Exodus 12–16)
- Make sandstorm pictures of the Bible story. Remind kids that God is real. God can do all things.

- Jesus and the Woman at the Well (John 4:6-11,19-30,39-42)
- Make sandstorm pictures of the Bible story. Remind kids that Jesus taught people what God is like.

- Ruth Helped Her Family (Ruth 1:22; 2:1-23)
- Make sandstorm pictures of the Bible story. Remind kids that God wants family members to help each other.

CREATION

Cause and Effect

Stand the blocks or dominoes on end, close enough that they will all fall after the first one is pushed forward.

Guide a child to gently push the first block down and watch the others fall. When the blocks have fallen, encourage kids to reset them in a wave pattern, standing them close enough for the falling action.

As they reposition the blocks, talk about choices kids make. Briefly tell the Bible story "Adam and Eve's Choice" (Genesis 2:7–3:23).

Ask kids what choice Adam and Eve made, then talk about right choices and what happens when someone makes a wrong choice.

- extra-thick dominoes or small, rectangular wood blocks

CHANGE IT UP!

- Elijah Prayed to God (1 Kings 18:1-2,41-46)
- God wants people to pray to Him.
- Encourage kids to talk about what happened in the Bible story.

- Jesus Calmed the Storm (Mark 4:1-2,35-41)
- Jesus has the power to perform miracles.
- Encourage kids to talk about what happened in the Bible story.

- Jesus and Bartimaeus (Mark 10:46-52)
- People can trust God to take care of them.
- Encourage kids to talk about what happened in the Bible story.

- copy paper
- watercolors
- paintbrushes
- cups of water

Creation Creations

- Tell kids that *create* means "to make something."
- Encourage kids to use the supplies to paint the story of God's creation. Remind them to carefully rinse their brushes in water before painting with a new color.
- As they paint, share the Bible story "God Created the World" (Genesis 1:1–2:3). Mention that kids should thank God for His beautiful creation.

CHANGE IT UP!

- Jesus Was Born (Luke 2:1-20)
- God sent Jesus to earth because He loves people.
- Paint the manger scene.

- Miriam's Family (Exodus 2:1-10)
- God wants families to worship together.
- Paint Moses' family.

- The Man Who Said Thank You (Luke 17:11-19)
- God wants people to pray.
- Paint the Bible story.

Drop the Clothespin

Encourage each child to hold a clothespin at nose level and give an example of a right or wrong choice. Challenge kids to drop their clothespins into the corresponding jars.

Tell the Bible story "Adam and Eve's Choice" (Genesis 2:7–3:23). Remind kids that the Bible tells people to do what is right and good.

CHANGE IT UP!

- People Welcomed Jesus (Matthew 21:1-11,14-16)
- Jesus wants people to love and obey Him.

- Joseph Showed Love (Genesis 45:1-11,16-28; 46:28-34; 47:1-11)
- People can show love to their families.

- David and Jonathan (1 Samuel 14:49; 18:1-4; 20)
- People's choices can make them happy or sad.

- clothespins
- 2 widemouthed plastic jars—Use mailing labels to label separate jars: *right choice* and *wrong choice.*

CREATION

Indoor Campout

- sleeping bags or blankets
- small tent or blanket-covered table
- flashlights

- Encourage kids to pretend to camp. As they play, comment that people enjoy spending time outside in the world God created. Name other family activities that can be done outdoors.
- Invite kids to rest in the tent. Tell the Bible story "God Created the World" (Genesis 1:1–2:3).
- Tell them that when God created the world and everything in it, He saw everything He had made, and it was very good. Kids can thank God for the beautiful world.

CHANGE IT UP!

- Breakfast with Jesus (John 21:1-17)
- Jesus enjoyed spending time with His friends.

- The People Built the Tabernacle (Exodus 35:4-21; 36:1-3)
- At church people have different kinds of jobs.

- Aquila and Priscilla (Acts 18:1-4,18-28)
- God wants people to work together.

Wash Animal Figures

Pour a small amount of water in the dishpan. Set the dishpan on the towel.
Guide older kids to take turns washing and drying the animals. As they work, talk about the animals God made.
Show babies the animals, identify their names, and tell them that God made the animals.
Tell the Bible story "God Created the World" (Genesis 1:1–2:3). Point out that God created the world and all kinds of animals. Encourage kids to thank God for animals.

- plastic dishpan
- towel
- paper towels
- age-appropriate vinyl or plastic animal figures

- God Cared for Noah (Genesis 6–9)
- God cares and provides for people.

- Jesus Was Born (Luke 2:1-20)
- God sent Jesus to earth because He loves people.

- Abram Moved to a New Home (Genesis 12:1-9)
- People show love for God by obeying Him.

CREATION

SCIENCE & Nature

- rice—Place in a plastic dishpan.
- plastic scoops
- measuring cups
- small kitchen scale

JESUS

FAMILY

CHURCH

CREATION

Rice Remedy

- Encourage kids to scoop and pour the rice.
- Allow them to pour rice into the scale container and see how much it weighs. Help kids identify the numbers on the scale and measuring cups.
- Tell the Bible story "A Church Helped" (Acts 11:19-30). Explain that many people around the world eat rice daily. Thank God for the food He gives the children to eat.

CHANGE IT UP!

- Jesus Fed the People (John 6:1-13)
- Jesus performed miracles and healed the sick.

- Ruth Helped Her Family (Ruth 1:22; 2:1-23)
- God wants families to work together.

- Jesus' Special Supper (Matthew 26:17-30)
- The Lord's Supper is a special meal to remember Jesus.

exturized Artwork

Demonstrate how to lay a sheet of paper over a nature item and rub the long side of a crayon back and forth over the paper. The texture of the item under the paper will form a picture where the crayon wax is deposited.

Guide kids to create texture rubbings with the nature items. Remind kids of the Bible story "God Made the World" (Genesis 1:1–2:3). Talk about seeing textures and details in the world God made.

- copy paper
- crayons with their wrappings removed
- flat nature items with different textures (leaves, pressed flowers, flat rocks, and so forth)

CHANGE IT UP!

Jesus Is Alive (John 20:1-18)
- Jesus died on the cross and is alive!
- Use nature items to create "Jesus Is Alive!" artwork.

The Good Samaritan (Luke 10:25-37)
- People can make right choices.
- Use nature items to create a picture of the Bible story.

- A Woman Gave an Offering (Mark 12:41-44)
- At church people have different kinds of jobs.
- Use nature items to create a picture of people at church.

CREATION

SCIENCE & Nature

- magnifying glasses
- waxed paper
- seeds—Choose several varieties, including birdseed and plant seed.

Seed Exploring

- Allow boys and girls to place seeds on waxed paper. Invite them to use magnifying glasses to look at the seeds.
- Encourage kids to tell the differences between birdseed and plant seed.
- Share that the Bible says God will help people. God cares for everyone. He shows that He cares by giving people a place to live, food, clothing, and love.
- Option: Allow kids to take some birdseed outside and feed birds.

CHANGE IT UP!

- Jesus Fed the People (John 6:1-13)
- Jesus showed love by helping people.

- Joseph Showed Love (Genesis 45:1-11,16-28; 46:28-34; 47:1-11)
- People can show love to their families.

- Ruth Helped Her Family (Ruth 1:22; 2:1-23)
- People's choices can make them happy or sad.

Super Duper Somethings
from Almost Absolutely Nothing

FOUR USES FOR A BOX

1. *Use as a doll bed.* Cover a shoe box with colored contact plastic (if desired). Place a doll and a small blanket in the box. Lay the box on the floor near a child-sized rocking chair, if available.
2. *Make a parking garage.* Turn a box on its side. Draw lines along the box side to create parking spaces. The child can "drive" cars into the box and park them between the lines.
3. *Make a tunnel.* Open the ends of a large appliance box to make a tunnel for the children. Place pictures along the inside walls for children to view as they crawl through the tunnel, or place an item at one end to entice a younger preschooler to crawl through the tunnel.
4. *Make blocks.* Stuff several boxes (various sizes) with newspaper and seal with wide tape. Cover the boxes with colored contact plastic. Encourage children to use the blocks for building. For additional fun, cut self-adhesive Velcro® into 2-inch strips. Attach a Velcro piece to the outside top and bottom of each box. Children will enjoy attaching and separating boxes.

FOUR USES FOR A CARDBOARD TUBE

1. *Make a shaker.* Place ribbon strands inside one end of a cardboard tube. Staple the end closed so strands dangle out. Pour aquarium gravel, rice, or other material into the tube. Place additional ribbon strands into the open end and staple closed. Cover with colored contact plastic or decorate as desired.
2. *Make pretend binoculars.* Place two small cardboard tubes side by side. Hold tubes in place and wrap tape around them (or use hot glue between them). Decorate as desired.
3. *Make a moving streamer.* Tape several crepe paper pieces to one end of a cardboard tube. Cover the tube with colored contact plastic. Children can wave the streamers to music.
4. *Cut circles in play dough.* Provide small cardboard tubes and play dough. Children may enjoy making circle shapes or cutting out "cookies."

FOUR USES FOR A ZIPLOCK BAG

1. *Protect a teaching picture.* Slide a teaching picture into a large ziplock bag. Seal the bag. If necessary, tape the end of the bag with masking tape. The picture will be protected during a water activity or other messy play.

2. *Finger-paint.* Pour thin tempera paint into a ziplock freezer bag. Squeeze the air out of the bag. Seal the bag, then tape closed with transparent tape. Children can lay the freezer bag on a table and "finger-paint" designs (with no messy hands).

3. *Make a book.* Stack four quart-sized freezer ziplock bags, open edge at the top. Punch holes on the left sides of the bags. Tie bags together with yarn. Mount pictures on poster board, trimmed to fit in bags. Slip pictures in the bags. Change pictures for a new book!

4. *Make a mini terrarium.* Dip a few cotton balls in water. Drop wet cotton balls into a sandwich-sized ziplock bag. Sprinkle grass seed into the bag (on the cotton balls). Seal the bag and tape it to a window. The grass seed should sprout in a few days.

FOUR USES FOR A CLEAR PLASTIC BOTTLE

1. *Use with water play.* Cut the top portion from a bottle (about ¼-inch after bottle widens). Cover cut edges with tape. Use the top portion as a funnel and the bottom portion as a pouring cup. Use small uncut bottles in water play.

2. *Make a musical instrument.* Place several jingle bells into a clean bottle. Seal the lid with glue and wide transparent tape.

3. *Make a viewing bottle.* Fill a bottle halfway with sand. Add coins, foam shapes, or alphabet beads. You can also add small pictures, words, numbers, or letters on pieces of index card. Seal the top. Shake to hide the items in the sand. Provide a list of items to find within the bottle.

4. *Make an ocean bottle.* Fill a bottle halfway with water. Add blue food color until water is light to medium blue. Add baby oil or mineral oil to about 1 inch above the water line. Seal lid with glue and wide clear tape.

R. Scott Wiley

CHAPTER 5
Family

About the LOBL Concept Area: Family

Families come in all shapes and sizes. Some live together in one house, some live apart. Some have a mom and a dad, some don't. Some have sisters and brothers, some don't. Some have grandparents, others don't. But no matter what the makeup, families are important.

A child's life experience will have great impact on his concept of what a family should be. As my own family has encountered changes through the years, I have discovered—even taken comfort in knowing—that there is no perfect family. Today's world can be uncertain. Families are crumbling all around us. Children need security. How can we help? We can share God's plan for families.

Helping a preschooler know that God gave him a family is an important step in a child's understanding that God has a plan for his life. By including activities and Bible stories that portray family members who love and respect each other, serve others, and worship together, we can help a child begin to understand God's design for the family.

Through simple actions such as encouraging a child to draw a picture, providing time for role play, reading books about grandparents, or working a puzzle of a family at mealtime, you can provide learning opportunities that will reinforce a biblical view of families.

As you teach, be sure to consider each child's home environment and know that you can and will make a difference in their lives.

Klista Storts

Important Note About Allergies:

When working with preschoolers it is important to always be aware of allergies. When using this book in a classroom setting, please print the allergy alert from the CD-ROM and inform parents of ingredients or nature items used in the activity.

Helper Handprints

Mix the plaster of paris as directed on the container. Pour the mixture onto the plate. Let it set for a few minutes.

Form a loop with ribbon and press the loose ends securely into the top edge of the plaster.

Invite a child to spread his fingers. Help him press his hand into the plaster to form his handprint.

Invite older children to decorate their handprints by inserting floral marbles. Place the plaster mold aside to dry.

While working, tell the Bible story "Ruth Helped Her Family" (Ruth 1:22; 2:1-23). Discuss ways kids can use their hands to help others.

Tell each child that God made his family.

CHANGE IT UP!

- God Promised Abraham and Sarah a Baby (Genesis 12:2-3; 17)
- God always keeps His promises.

- Jesus Was Born (Luke 2:1-20)
- God sent Jesus to earth because He loves people.

- Jesus and Bartimaeus (Mark 10:46-52)
- People can trust God to care for them.

- insulated foam plates
- plaster of paris
- water
- floral marbles
- stirring spoon
- plastic container for mixing
- thin ribbon— Cut into 6-inch lengths.

FAMILY

Clay People

- colored modeling clay
- rolling pins
- buttons
- unsharpened pencils

- Place rolling pins, unsharpened pencils, and buttons on the table. Invite each child to make clay people to represent the members of her family.
- Guide kids to use unsharpened pencils to form facial features and buttons to decorate their clay persons.
- As kids work, tell the Bible story "Abraham, Sarah, and Isaac" (Genesis 18:1-15; 21:1-3).
- Share that God planned for people to live in families. God made Isaac to be in Abraham and Sarah's family. God did what He had promised to do. He gave Abraham a family.

CHANGE IT UP!

- People Welcomed Jesus (Matthew 21:1-11,14-16)
- Jesus is God's one and only Son.

- God Created Man and Woman (Genesis 2:7–3:23)
- God gave people the ability to make choices.

- The People Read the Bible (Acts 17:1-4,10-12)
- People at church pray, worship, give, sing, read the Bible, and listen to teaching and preaching.

FAMILY

- chalkboard
- chalk
- eraser

Chalk It Up

Briefly tell kids the Bible story "Timothy Learned About God" (Acts 16:1-3; 2 Timothy 1:1-5; 3:14-17). Comment that Timothy's mother and grandmother taught him about Jesus. Encourage kids to use the chalk to draw their families on the chalkboard.

- As kids draw, comment that God wants parents to teach their children about God.

CHANGE IT UP!

- Hezekiah and the People Thanked God (2 Chronicles 29)
- God wants people to worship Him.

- Jesus Was Born (Luke 2:1-20)
- God sent Jesus to earth because He loves people.

- The Church Chose Special Helpers (Acts 6:1-7)
- Churches provide ways for people to help each other.

FAMILY

- transportation toys
  (boats, cars, trucks,
  airplanes, donkeys,
  camels, oxen, and
  so forth)

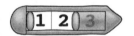

On the Go

- Arrange the toys on the floor. Invite kids to explore the transportation toys.
- As kids play, share that the Bible says, "Since you were a child, you have learned from the Bible." Briefly tell the Bible story "Timothy Learned About God" (Acts 16:1-3; 2 Timothy 1:1-5; 3:14-17).
- Tell kids that parents can teach their children about God and Jesus when they are traveling.

CHANGE IT UP!

- Wise Men Worshiped Jesus (Matthew 2:1-12)
- God sent Jesus to earth because He loves people.

- Abram Moved to a New Home (Genesis 12:1-9)
- People show love for God by obeying Him.

- Jesus' Family Went to Church (Luke 2:22-40)
- People at church worship, pray, give, sing, read the Bible, and listen to teaching and preaching.

amily Collage

Distribute paper and magazine pictures. Invite kids to choose pictures of families to put on their pages.

Help kids glue the pictures onto the paper. As they work, talk about their family members. Share with kids that God knows everything about them. He gave each child a family to love and care for him.

Encourage kids to use markers and crayons to decorate their collages. Tell the Bible story "The First Family" (Genesis 1–4).

- white paper
- crayons
- washable markers
- glue stick
- magazine pictures of families

CHANGE IT UP!

- Mary and Martha (Luke 10:38-42)
- Jesus taught people what God is like.

- Ruth Helped Her Family (Ruth 1:22; 2:1-23)
- People's choices can make them happy or sad.

- Andrew Told His Brother About Jesus (John 1:35-42)
- Missionaries tell people about God and Jesus.

FAMILY

Ice Cream in a Coffee Can

HOME LIVING

- "Coffee Can Ice Cream Recipe" (CD-ROM)
- half-gallon milk
- 1 can sweetened condensed milk
- 9-ounce whipped topping
- empty 1-pound coffee can with lid
- empty 3-pound coffee can with lid
- ice cubes
- rock salt
- paper towels
- mixing spoon
- masking tape
- napkins
- bowls or cups
- spoons
- dish towel (optional)

- Briefly share the Bible story "Jesus Healed a Sick Woman" (Mark 1:29-31).
- Lead and assist in the following steps on the "Coffee Can Ice Cream Recipe" (CD-ROM):
- Allow kids to take turns rolling the can back and forth for six minutes. Open the larger can and add more ice and salt.
- Seal the can again and continue rolling the can for six more minutes.
- Invite kids to talk about times they have been sick and to name what they used or did to feel better. Share that God loves and cares for families.
- Open both cans. Serve the ice cream.

CHANGE IT UP!

- Jesus Taught About God's Care (Matthew 5:1-2; 6:25-34)
- God cares and provides for people.

- God Created the World (Genesis 1:1–2:3)
- God wants people to thank Him for His creation.
- Remind kids that they used ingredients to make ice cream; God made the world from nothing!

CHURCH

- Paul Told Lydia About Jesus (Acts 16:11-15)
- People at church tell others about Jesus.
- Consider telling people about Jesus at an ice cream party.

eel Sensory Bags

Prepare the bags by filling each with hair styling gel. Seal each bag with glue and a strip of duct tape. Chill some of the bags in a refrigerator and place others in a warm window or under a warm light.

Place the prepared bags on the table along with the "Hot and Cold Items" pictures.

Encourage kids to sort the pictures into two groups: hot and cold. As kids sort, briefly share the Bible story "Jesus Healed a Sick Woman" (Mark 1:29-31). Point out that the woman in the story was sick with a fever. When a person has a fever, she feels very hot. Invite each child to touch the warm bag.

Invite kids to squeeze and squish the bags to experiment with the differences in temperature.

Emphasize that the woman in the story did not stay hot. Jesus held her hands for a few moments and helped her up! She was not sick anymore, and she no longer had a fever. God took care of Simon's mother-in-law. God is good to everyone.

CHANGE IT UP!

- Elisha and the Shunammite Woman (2 Kings 4:8-37)
- God heals people.

- Jesus and Bartimaeus (Mark 10:46-52)
- Jesus performed miracles and healed the sick.

- The Good Samaritan (Luke 10:25-37)
- People can make right choices.

- ziplock freezer bags
- hair gel
- glue
- duct tape
- scissors
- "Hot and Cold Items" (CD-ROM)

FAMILY

Tissue Corsages

- tissue paper or 2-ply colored facial tissue—Stack at least 5 sheets of tissue for each child.
- chenille stems— Cut each stem in half, providing one-half stem for each project.
- Make a sample corsage.

- Guide each child to fold a stack of tissue into an accordion or fan shape.
- Demonstrate how to wrap the chenille stem around the middle of the accordion-folded piece and close stem ends together.
- Lead kids to pull up each layer to the top center, one layer at a time.
- Explain that kids can be thankful for the Bible. They can be thankful for their families and friends who teach them the Bible. Encourage each child to show his thankfulness by giving his corsage as a gift to someone who helps him.
- Tell the Bible story "Timothy Learned About God" (Acts 16:1-3; 2 Timothy 1:1-5; 3:14-17). Remind kids to be thankful for their families.

CHANGE IT UP!

- Wise Men Worshiped Jesus (Matthew 2:1-12)
- God sent Jesus to earth because He loves people.

- God Created the World (Genesis 1:1–2:3)
- God created the world and everything in it.

- Paul Told Lydia About Jesus (Acts 16:11-15)
- People at church tell others about Jesus.

FAMILY

DRAMATIC PLAY

Drawing Blueprints

Place items on the table. Briefly tell the Bible story "Elisha's Room" (2 Kings 4:8-10). Point out that the couple helped God's people in need. Tell kids they can help people in need.

Prompt boys and girls to describe some of the furniture items a person might place in a room.

Invite kids to play with the tools.

Encourage them to experiment with the measuring tape by measuring different items in the classroom.

Explain that people who build rooms, buildings, and furniture begin with plans called blueprints. Show "Blueprint" (CD-ROM). Invite kids to make their own blueprints. Guide them to draw with the chalk on the blue paper.

- chalk
- blue construction paper
- play tools (plastic measuring tape, ruler, play tool kit)
- "Blueprint" (CD-ROM)

CHANGE IT UP!

- Jesus Healed A Paralyzed Man (Mark 2:1-12)
- God shows His love to all people.
- Guide kids to draw a picture of the hole in the roof.

God

- The People Built the Tabernacle (Exodus 35:4-21; 36:1-3)
- At church people have different kinds of jobs.
- Guide kids to draw pictures of the church.

CHURCH

- A Church Helped (Acts 11:19-30)
- People's offerings help missionaries in their communities and around the world.
- Guide kids to draw pictures of people helping.

COMMUNITY & WORLD

FAMILY

- scissors
- assorted gloves (carpenter's, gardening, mittens, dress gloves)
- "Gloves" (CD-ROM)— Print two or more copies and cut apart.

"Helping Hands" Game

- Set the assorted gloves (unmatched) on a table. Place the pictures facedown on the table.
- Explain that today kids are going to play "Helping Hands." During this game, kids will match gloves and talk about ways people who wear each type of glove might use their hands to help others.
- Review the Bible story "David Helped His Family" (1 Samuel 16:11-12; 17:12-22).
- Encourage boys and girls to try on the gloves once they match and sort all the gloves.
- Comment that the Bible says to help God's people in need. Discuss how kids can help people.

CHANGE IT UP!

- Mary and Martha (Luke 10:38-42)
- Jesus taught people what God is like.

- God Took Care of Noah and the Animals (Genesis 6–9)
- God provides for His creation.

- The Church Chose Special Helpers (Acts 6:1-7)
- Churches provide ways for people to help one another.

FAMILY

Preparing Your Child for Thought-Igniting Learning

It was a typical Sunday morning at our house. My husband and I were trying to get to Sunday School on time with our two-year-old daughter. As we pulled out of the driveway our daughter began saying, "Bible, Bible." I was so proud that she understood we were on our way to church to learn about the Bible! Then it hit me: *In the rush, what had I done with my Bible? I had set it on top of the car!* Our daughter was trying to tell me she could see my Bible flying off the car and onto the road! After retrieving my Bible I began to wonder if we had we done everything to prepare her for a good experience at church? Or were we so rushed that she didn't understand the importance of what we were doing? There are many things parents and teachers can do to prepare preschoolers for learning at church.

PREPARE YOUR HEART

Parents: Preschoolers learn by watching and imitating what we do. The best way you can teach them about God is to grow in your own relationship with Him. As you draw closer to God, your kids will see the results in your life. Sometimes you may feel you don't have time for personal prayer and study because your family needs you for so many things, but it is vital.

Teachers: Spending time in personal prayer and Bible study makes better teachers. When you have a growing personal relationship with God, it comes out in everything said and done in the classroom. When you feel comfortable with the Bible you can focus on spending quality time in class.

BE ORGANIZED

Parents: Prepare for Sunday just as you do for a work/school day. Lay out clothes the night before. Go to bed on time and have something nutritious and manageable planned for breakfast. A little planning can make Sunday morning flow smoothly. Then your preschooler can better focus on the Bible study session and understand that church is a priority for your family.

Teachers: Make sure your room is safe and prepared for the session before preschoolers arrive. Then you can give your full attention to the children and begin building relationships with them. Kids get excited when they come into a room with the activities waiting for them. Not having to stress over last-minute details will give you the opportunity to enjoy time with them.

HAVE MEANINGFUL CONVERSATION

Parents: Take some time on Saturday night to talk about what you are going to be doing at church on Sunday. Remind kids why you go to church and what they can learn about in the Bible. Pray for your child's Sunday School teachers and get excited about the next morning.

Teachers: Focus on more than the activity. Take time to relate it to the Bible story and make the life application. Preschoolers need to take away more than just the activity. Make the connection to God's Word. Find ways to relate the story to their individual lives as you talk with them.

REVIEW THE DAY

Parents: Make a point of asking your children what they did in Sunday School. They may not remember everything, but if you initiate the conversation it will help reinforce what they have learned. Look at the take-home page and complete some of the suggested activities with your child. Look for ways during the week to relate the Bible story and life application to your family.

Teachers: Take time to review the session. What were the best things that happened? Make notes about what went well and what you would do differently. Improvements are always possible, so take time to think about it. It will help you be more successful in your session the next week.

Preschoolers will learn so much more when you are prepared and give them the tools they need to make the most of their time in church. God is faithful to bless all of your efforts, but you do need to give Him your best to honor Him in the work He has given you.

Valerie Davidson

CHAPTER 6
Self

SELF

About the LOBL Concept Area: Self

Matthew and Ella worked side by side in Sunday School. Suddenly Matthew complained, "She just called me ugly! That is not loving one another!"

I looked at Ella. I could almost see the sparks flying around her head as she quickly thought up a defense.

"I didn't say 'ugly,' I said 'lov-e-ly,'" she drawled as she met my look with a challenging stare. What a teachable moment! Together, the three of us reviewed the Bible verse for the session, "Do all you can to get along with others." (Romans 12:18) Out of this conversation Matthew, Ella, and I were able to talk about ways to show love for friends and recognize times when we might hurt them. Ella surprised me before the end of our conversation by stating: "I really did say 'ugly.' I was mad because Matthew was using the big spoon and I wanted it." With little prompting, Ella apologized to Matthew before the two children returned to their play.

The concept area of *Self* is a natural area for preschool children to explore and learn about the Bible. Be sure to include activities that help each child make a life application from the Bible.

Kathy Collins

Important Note About Allergies:

When working with preschoolers it is important to always be aware of allergies. When using this book in a classroom setting, please print the allergy alert from the CD-ROM and inform parents of ingredients or nature items used in the activity.

SELF

Samuel's Socks

Tell the Bible story "Young Samuel" (1 Samuel 1:1-28; 2:18-21,26).
Place the socks on the floor.
Invite a child to pull a sock over her foot. Comment that the Bible
says that God made people. God made kids to grow and learn.
Kids can learn at church.

• adult-size socks

Discover Musical Sounds

MUSIC & BOOKS

- Put a small amount of jingle bells, rice, or dry beans in each bottle.
- Use tape and a hot glue gun to secure the lids on the bottles.
- Hide the bottles beneath a small blanket or towel.
- Encourage a crawling baby to discover the bottles under the blanket and roll or shake them to hear a sound.
- Say that people can sing songs to God. They can say, "Thank You, God, for making me special."

• three plastic bottles
• jingle bells
• rice or dry beans
• hot glue gun
• tape
• small baby blanket or towel

Play a Sound Game

MUSIC & BOOKS

- Place the sound-making items in the bag.
- Encourage a child to remove each item, look at it, and discover the sound it makes.
- Hide the items under a towel.
- Remove one item and place it in the bag. Then shake the bag to make the sound of that item. Invite the child to guess which item matches the sound.
- Say that God gave people ears so they can hear different sounds. God can hear us when we talk to Him.

• towel
• large paper bag
• sound-making items (jingle bells, set of keys, and so forth)

SELF

SCIENCE & Nature

- scissors
- inflatable balls
- bubble solution
- bubble wands
- eye droppers
- containers for bubble solution and water
- straws wrapped in paper
- sponge animal capsules
- dry sponges— Cut into various small shapes.

Growing, Growing, Grown!

- Briefly tell the Bible story "Samuel's Birth and Dedication" (1 Samuel 1:20-28).
- Display the materials. Invite kids to take turns making straw wrappers grow by accordion-folding the papers then dropping water on them, immersing sponges in water, inflating balls, and blowing bubbles.
- As children explore, comment that seeing these items getting bigger reminds them that God planned for Samuel to grow. God planned for kids to grow.

CHANGE IT UP!

- God Took Care of Noah (Genesis 6–9)
- God provides for His creation.

- God Created the World (Genesis 1:1–2:3)
- God created the earth and everything in it.

- Baby Moses (Exodus 2:1-10)
- Family members love one another.

SELF

DRAMATIC PLAY

Growing Limbo

Briefly tell the Bible story "Samuel's Birth and Dedication" (1 Samuel 1:20-28).
- Select two kids to hold the rod or broom, one at each end.
- Hold the rod about 10 inches off the ground. Each child will have a chance to go under the rod.
- Change rod holders and instruct the new rod holders to raise the rod up a little. Continue the game, raising the rod and alternating rod holders each round.
- Emphasize that God is with kids in everything they do. God has plans for all people to grow. As kids grow older, they are able to do many more things.

- broom or shower curtain rod

CHANGE IT UP!

- Jesus Showed Love to Zacchaeus (Luke 19:1-10)
- Remind kids that Zacchaeus was a short man.
- Tell kids that Jesus is the example of how to live.

- Timothy Learned About God (Acts 16:1-3; 2 Timothy 1:1-5; 3:14-17)
- The Bible helps people know what God wants them to do.
- Remind kids that Timothy studied the Bible as he grew older.

- Jesus' Family Went to Church (Luke 2:22-40)
- God wants families to go to church together.
- Remind kids that Jesus learned more about God as He grew older.

SELF

Right or Wrong

- markers
- masking tape
- paper grocery bags—Write *Wrong* on one bag and *Right* on the other.
- index cards—Write the following on separate cards: *Listen to my parents; Hit a friend; Pray; Take a toy away from a friend; Do my chores; Do not take turns on the playground.* Make several sets.

- Use masking tape to create two start lines on the floor.
- Form two teams. Direct each team to stand behind a start line.
- Invite kids to take turns walking quickly to the pile of cards. Each child should pick one card and decide if the choice on the card is a right choice or wrong choice. He will place the card in the corresponding bag.
- Assist kids with staying in line and taking turns. Direct each child to return to the end of the line after his turn.
- Tell the Bible story "Daniel and His Friends" (Daniel 1:1-20). Daniel and his friends made the right choice. Kids can choose to make right choices.

CHANGE IT UP!

- Adam and Eve Made a Choice (Genesis 2:7–3:23)
- God loves people even when they make wrong choices.

- Mary and Martha (Luke 10:38-42)
- Jesus taught people what God is like.

- A Church Helped (Acts 11:19-30)
- People can be a part of God's work.

Good Choice Trains

Tell the Bible story "Daniel and His Friends" (Daniel 1:1-20).
Point out that Daniel chose to do what was right.
Invite kids to make right choice trains. Distribute index cards and display the prepared paper. Guide each child to write *I can choose to make right choices* on one side of her cards. (For younger children, perform this task prior to the activity.) Write one word per card.
On the other side of each card, encourage each child to draw a picture of herself or other people making right choices.
Help kids punch one hole on each end of their cards.
Direct them to lay their cards on the table in the correct order.
Assist kids in tying the cards together with yarn to create good choice trains.
Remind kids that, like Daniel, they can choose to make right choices.

- scissors
- markers
- yarn
- hole punch
- index cards—Cut each card in half.
- embellishments such as sequins or stickers
- paper—In large letters, write *I can choose to make right choices*.

CHANGE IT UP!

- Jesus Is Alive (John 20:1-18)
- Guide kids to write *Jesus died on the cross and is alive!*

- God Created Man and Woman (Genesis 2:7–3:23)
- Guide kids to write *I can make good choices!*

- Joseph Obeyed His Father (Genesis 37:12-17)
- Guide kids to write *I can obey my parents!*

SELF

Mystery Bag Building

- building items
  (interlocking blocks,
  building blocks,
  wooden blocks, craft
  sticks, PVC pipes and
  joints, play dough)
- large grocery bags—
  Place building items
  in separate bags. Set
  the bags on the floor.

- Tell the Bible story "Nehemiah Rebuilt the Walls"
  (Nehemiah 2:18; 3:1-2).
- Lead each child to choose a bag and find a place in the room
  to stand.
- Direct kids to open their bags and build something with the items
  in the bags.
- Allow a few minutes for kids to build, then encourage kids to
  exchange mystery bags with a friend and build something new.
- Challenge kids to build specific items at different rotations
  (a wall, tower, building, gate, and so forth).
- Remind kids that Nehemiah prayed, asking God to help him do
  everything. Kids can pray and ask God to help them obey Him.

CHANGE IT UP!

- People Found a Lost Bible Scroll (2 Kings 22:1-13; 23:1-3)
- The stories in the Bible are true.

CHURCH

- The People Built the Tabernacle (Exodus 35:4-21; 36:1-3)
- At church people have different kinds of jobs.

- A Church Helped (Acts 11:19-30)
- People can be a part of God's work.

Decorate Footprints

Review the Bible story "Simeon Praised God" (Luke 2:25-35).
Guide each child to stand on a piece of construction paper.
Lightly trace around her foot.
Encourage each child to cut out and decorate her footprint.
Assist the younger learners.
Distribute the Bible verse strips.
Direct kids to glue the strips to their footprints.
Talk about how the kids and their families travel to church.
Suggest that kids place their footprints in their bedrooms
as reminders that Jesus went to church.

- construction paper
- pencils
- markers
- scissors
- stickers
- glue sticks
- "Luke 2:27" (CD-ROM)—Print and copy as need. Cut apart.

CHANGE IT UP!

- The People Crossed the Jordan River (Joshua 3–4)
- God shows His love to all people.

- Jesus Taught About God's Care (Matthew 5:1-2; 6:25-34)
- Jesus taught people what God is like.

- God Created Man and Woman (Genesis 2:7–3:23)
- God created people with the ability to make choices.

SELF

Make Repairs

- yarn
- masking tape
- cardboard tubes
- cardboard pieces—
  Cut into the shape of
  planks of wood.

- Before the session, place the cardboard and tubes on the floor. Bend some of the cardboard and partially tear some of the tubes.
- Guide kids to help make repairs to the building materials. Show them how to use the tape or yarn to make the repairs.
- Tell the Bible story "Nehemiah" (Nehemiah 1:1-4; 2:1-8,17-18; 3).
- Comment that God helped Nehemiah know how to repair the wall. Tell kids that God can help them make right choices too.

CHANGE IT UP!

- People Found a Lost Bible Scroll (2 Kings 22:1-13; 23:1-3)
- The stories in the Bible are true.

CHURCH

- The People Built the Tabernacle (Exodus 35:4-21; 36:1-3)
- At church people have different kinds of jobs.

- A Church Helped (Acts 11:19-30)
- People help by giving offerings at church.

SELF

Nuts and Bolts

- Tell kids that nuts and bolts are used to keep pieces of wood or plastic together.
- Allow kids to sort the nuts and bolts in the muffin pans.
- Tell the Bible story "Nehemiah" (Nehemiah 1:1-4; 2:1-8,17-18; 3). Explain that Nehemiah and the people used tools to rebuild the wall.
- Comment that Nehemiah prayed and asked God to help him know what to do. Tell kids they can pray and ask God to help them obey.

- muffin pans or other divided containers
- a variety of nuts and bolts (metal and plastic)

CHANGE IT UP!

- God Cared for Noah (Genesis 6–9)
- God cares and provides for people.

- Abram and Lot (Genesis 13:1-12,14-18)
- God wants families to work together.

- The People Built the Tabernacle (Exodus 35:4-21; 36:1-3)
- At church people have different kinds of jobs.

SELF

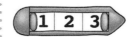

1 2 3

Scrub Vegetables

- plastic trays
- index cards
- marker
- toothbrushes or vegetable brushes
- small bowl of water
- paper towels
- Bible times vegetables (peas, beans, lentils, green onions, potatoes, carrots, parsnips, cucumbers, lettuce)

- Arrange the vegetables on plastic trays. Write the name of each vegetable on an index card.
- Tell the Bible story "Daniel Chose Good Food" (Daniel 1:1-20).
- Display the vegetables. Explain that people in Bible times ate these kinds of vegetables.
- Invite kids to dip toothbrushes into the bowl of water then use them to wash the vegetables. Invite older kids to match each vegetable to its name. Let babies touch the vegetables. Tell them: "God made food for you."
- Comment that God loves people and provides vegetables to eat to keep bodies healthy. Point out that eating the healthy food God provides is one way kids can obey Him.

CHANGE IT UP!

- Mary and Martha (Luke 10:38-42)
- Jesus taught people what God is like.

- God Created the World (Genesis 1:1–2:3)
- God created the world and everything in it.

- Ruth Took Care of Her Family (Ruth 1:22; 2:1-23)
- Family members love one another.

SELF

Igniting & Exciting Ways to Guide Behavior

Whining, crying, hitting, and biting! What can I do? Is there a way to avoid or minimize the difficult behaviors often seen in my preschool-age children? While there is not a simple answer, there are some things we can do to help. Let's take a look at three areas that influence our ability to guide the behavior of preschool children.

PHYSICAL NEEDS

When I am physically tired, I am irritable, impatient, and find it difficult to focus. Can you expect any less from a preschooler? A mother once expressed concern to me about her 4-year-old daughter's behavior toward her siblings. I asked the mother about the amount of sleep her daughter received. She commented that her daughter didn't get to bed until around 11 p.m. each night. This child was receiving only about 8 hours of sleep each night, yet preschool children require 11-13 hours. The key to managing this child's behavior may include an earlier bedtime.

A child with unmet physical needs is likely to display any number of difficult behaviors. Preschool children often lack not only the ability to reason, but the ability to verbally inform you of a need. It is your responsibility to anticipate and meet these needs. Doing so can avoid behaviors that are a direct result of an unmet physical need.

DEVELOPMENTAL CHARACTERISTICS

"I will praise You, because I have been remarkably and wonderfully made." (Psalm 139:14) Luke 2:52 states, "And Jesus increased in wisdom and stature and in favor with God and with people." God desires for people to view children as His remarkable creations and to see the plan He has for kids to grow and develop in all areas of development.

Developmental characteristics are not excuses but rather reasons for some behaviors in young children. One-year-olds are movers and shakers. Two-year-olds are realizing they can exert some control and three-year-olds develop fears. Four-year-olds love language and nonsense while five-year-olds are rule makers. Each developmental stage brings its own set of characteristics.

ENVIRONMENT

There is a store in my community that sells name brand clothing at discounted prices. I rarely go into this store because it is cluttered and unorganized. The shelves are messy and the layout of the store is confusing.

Adults can choose to not shop or dine in an environment that is frustrating. Preschoolers don't get a choice. Clutter, too many toys and activities, and a poorly arranged schedule can overwhelm and frustrate a preschooler. When a preschooler gets overwhelmed or frustrated, he may display the behaviors you are trying to manage or control.

Understand that young children sometimes use behavior as a means of communication. Listen to what your child's behavior is saying. Is a crowded schedule rushing you through meals and activities? Are your expectations unrealistic? Is the environment cluttered and unorganized?

When you begin to recognize changes and improvements you need to make, don't try to tackle it all at once. You may get overwhelmed and not make any changes at all! Try journaling for several days. Write down any difficult behaviors and what was happening before, during, and after the behavior occurred. Make note of any known or suspected unmet physical needs. Challenge yourself to understand what is going on developmentally. After several days, read over the journal to see if you find any common repetitions. Choose one or two changes to work on at one time. Be consistent in making these changes. Above all else, remember to seek God's guidance as you work to guide the behavior of preschool children.

Debbie Miller

CHAPTER 7

Church

About the LOBL Concept Area: Church

"God, are you in here?" I heard this question one Sunday after the morning services. I discovered 3-year-old Alex and his mom going from classroom to classroom. Alex's mom told me he was convinced God was here somewhere since he was in God's house. The family had a habit of calling church *God's house*, instead of *church*. Alex was confused. It was the perfect teaching moment for Alex and his mom. I was able to help Alex's mom know how to use words Alex could understand.

It is important for preschoolers to receive strong foundations in understanding what the church is and does. Children can be taught, "People at church love and teach me," as babies, then "Churches are part of God's plan for people," as kindergartners. Kids can begin to learn about worship as well. They can learn that people sing, talk to God, listen to Bible stories, give money, and read the Bible at church. By establishing strong foundations, you will help preschoolers learn to enjoy going to church and to ultimately desire to attend.

Tracey Rogers

CHRUCH

Important Note About Allergies:

When working with preschoolers it is important to always be aware of allergies. When using this book in a classroom setting, please print the allergy alert from the CD-ROM and inform parents of ingredients or nature items used in the activity.

Drive" to My Church

Draw a different "road" (zigzag, curvy, straight, and so forth) on each of the four strips of poster board. Place a picture of your church at the end of each road.

Prompt a child to follow a road with a toy car to get to church. Older preschoolers may wish to use interlocking blocks to build homes or other buildings along the roads.

Tell kids that people go to church because it is something God wants everyone to do. Share the Bible story "Jesus' Family Went to Church" (Luke 2:22-40).

 CHANGE IT UP!

The People Crossed the Jordan River (Joshua 3–4)
God shows His love to all people.

People Welcomed Jesus (Matthew 21:1-11,14-16)
Jesus wants people to love and obey Him.

Paul and Silas (Acts 16:22-32,34)
Missionaries tell people about God and Jesus.

- washable markers
- toy cars
- pictures of church
- interlocking blocks
- large piece of poster board—Cut into 4 strips.

CHURCH

Cleanup Time

- small brooms
- dust pans
- cleaning cloths

- Place the items on the floor.
- Invite kids to work together to clean the room. Tell them that people at church work together.
- Tell kids that they are helpers. Thank each child for being a helper at church.

CHANGE IT UP!

- Jesus Cooked for His Disciples (John 21:1-17)
- Jesus prepared a meal for His disciples.

- People Found a Lost Bible Scroll (2 Kings 22:1-13; 23:1-3)
- The stories in the Bible are true.

- Ruth Helped Her Family (Ruth 1:22; 2:1-23)
- Family members help one another.

Feel and Match Textures

Cut two 3-by-3-inch squares from several types of cloth. Place one square of each kind of cloth in the gift bag. Lay the remaining squares on the floor or table.
Invite a child to choose a cloth square, then encourage her to reach into the bag and feel the pieces of cloth without looking. See if she can pull out the square that matches the one she chose. Discuss the Bible story "Aquila and Priscilla" (Acts 18:1-4,18-28). Comment that people at church taught and told others about Jesus together.

- gift bag
- several types of cloth (different textures such as felt, burlap, velvet, and so forth)

CHANGE IT UP!

- God Took Care of Noah and the Animals (Genesis 6–9)
- God provides for His creation.
- Provide squares of steel wool, soft cotton, and leather.

- Daniel Obeyed God (Daniel 1:1-20)
- God wants people to do what He says.
- Place vegetables and fruits into the gift bag.

- A Church Helped (Acts 11:19-30)
- People show love by giving to others.
- Place wadded paper, cloth, and coins into the gift bag.

CHURCH

SCIENCE & Nature

- ziplock bags
- liquid starch, white glue—Mix ½ cup of each item together. Stir until it forms a ball. Knead it by hand until it is very smooth and no longer sticky.

God

Creation

Self

Play Putty Shapes

- Provide a clean covering for the table. Encourage kids to work the putty to make shapes of food items.
- Tell the Bible story "Breakfast with Jesus" (John 21:1-17). Lead kids to suggest what kinds of food Jesus prepared.
- Kids will enjoy the smooth and slippery feel of the putty. Store the putty in ziplock bags.

CHANGE IT UP!

- Joshua and Caleb Chose to Obey (Numbers 13:1-3,17-33; 14:1-10)
- God wants people to love and obey Him.

- God Took Care of Noah and the Animals (Genesis 6–9)
- God provides for His creation.

- Daniel Obeyed God (Daniel 1:1-20)
- God wants people to do what He says.

CHRUCH

Good "Scents" Ink

- paper
- craft sticks
- cotton swabs
- water
- instant fruit drink mix
- muffin tin

Distribute paper, craft sticks, and cotton swabs to each child.
Guide kids to take turns measuring 1 tablespoon drink mix
and 1 tablespoon water into each muffin tin space.
Invite kids to take turns mixing the "ink" by carefully stirring
with craft sticks.
Guide them to dip cotton swabs into the "ink" and write
and draw on their papers. As kids work, tell the Bible story
"Jeremiah Wrote About God" (Jeremiah 36:1-4).

- Tell kids that when the ink dries, they may smell it and remember
what fun they had today. Remind them that Baruch wrote down
the words from God. At church people learn about these words
from the Bible. People can read the Bible at church and at home.

CHANGE IT UP!

- God Gave the Ten Commandments (Exodus 19:1–20:21)
- God loves people even when they make wrong choices.
- Guide kids to use the ink to draw pictures of the Bible story.

- God Created the World (Genesis 1:1–2:3)
- God created the world and everything in it.
- Guide kids to use the ink to draw pictures of the Bible story.

- Aquila and Priscilla (Acts 18:1-4,18-28)
- God wants people to work together.
- Guide kids to use the ink to draw pictures of the Bible story.

CHURCH

Make Fruit Pizzas

- refrigerated sugar cookie dough
- 7 oz. marshmallow cream
- 8 oz. cream cheese
- baking sheet
- rolling pin
- bowl, large spoon
- plastic knives
- assorted fresh fruit— Cut into small pieces.

- Use a rolling pin to smooth the refrigerated sugar cookie dough into a single layer on an ungreased medium baking sheet. Bake according to the cookie directions.
- Blend the marshmallow cream and the cream cheese in a bowl.
- Guide kids to wash their hands and use the plastic knives to spread the marshmallow cream mixture over the sugar cookie crust.
- Invite kids to arrange the fruit on the pizza.
- Tell kids the Bible story "Jesus Fed the People" (John 6:1-13) while they work. Explain that Jesus showed love by helping people.

CHANGE IT UP!

- God Sent the People Food (Exodus 16:1-18)
- God cares for people's needs.

- Mary and Martha (Luke 10:38-42)
- Jesus taught people what God is like.

- Daniel Chose Good Food (Daniel 1:1-20)
- God wants people to do what He says.

CHRUCH

Play "Getting Ready for Church" Charades

Review "Simeon Praised God" (Luke 2:25-35) and remind kids that it is important to go to church to worship.
Invite kids to play a game about getting ready for church.
- Form two teams. Choose a volunteer to select a picture card and play out the action.
- Encourage the players on his team to guess what the child is doing. Continue alternating volunteers from each team to play out the pictures.
- Comment that Jesus' family went to church together. It was important to them to go to church. It is important that kids go to church. God wants families to go to church. At church, kids can learn more about Jesus.

CHANGE IT UP!

- Jesus Was Born (Luke 2:1-20)
- God sent Jesus to earth because He loves people.
- Create loving situations charade cards.

- David and Jonathan (1 Samuel 14:49; 18:1-4; 20)
- God wants people to love others.
- Create loving other charade cards.

- Paul and Barnabas Told About Jesus
  (Acts 13:1-5,13-16,32-33,42-51)
- Missionaries tell people about God and Jesus.
- Create helping situations charade cards.

- "Getting Ready for Church Charades" (CD-ROM)—Print and cut apart.

CHURCH

Make Place Mats

- 12-by-18-inch colored construction paper
- 9-by-12-inch white construction paper
- glue sticks
- markers
- clear contact plastic
- scissors
- "Bible Phrase Strips" (CD-ROM)—Print, copy, and cut apart.

- Invite each child to draw a picture on white construction paper of something he remembers about Jesus.
- Instruct each child to glue the completed picture onto a larger piece of colored construction paper.
- Tell kids they are making place mats to use at meal times.
- Instruct each child to glue a Bible phrase strip onto his place mat.
- Cover the place mats with clear contact plastic.
- Tell about "Jesus' Special Supper" (Matthew 26:17-30). At church, people have a special meal during worship time. This special meal is called the Lord's Supper. It is a time to remember what Jesus did.

CHANGE IT UP!

- Jesus Made Breakfast for His Disciples (John 21:1-17)
- Jesus performed miracles and healed the sick.

- Mary and Martha (Luke 10:38-42)
- God wants families to work together.

- Daniel Chose Good Food (Daniel 1:1-20)
- God wants people to obey Him.

CHRUCH

Make Friendship Bracelets

Assist kids in placing beads on the chenille stems to make friendship bracelets.

- Encourage each child to make one bracelet for a friend and one for herself.
- Ask boys and girls to identify people to whom they might give the bracelets.
- Review "Paul Told Lydia" (Acts 16:11-15) and talk about how important it is to tell friends about Jesus and invite them to church.

- chenille stems
- plastic bracelet beads

CHANGE IT UP!

- Peter and Cornelius (Acts 10:1-33)
- God shows His love to all people.

- David and Jonathan (1 Samuel 14:49; 18:1-4; 20)
- People's choices make them happy or sad.

- Aquila and Priscilla (Acts 18:1-4,18-28)
- God wants people to work together.

CHURCH

Make Painted Toast

- milk—Pour ¼ c. into each bowl.
- bread, butter
- juice
- food color
- plastic bowls
- spoons, cups
- pastry brushes
- plastic knives
- small paper plates
- napkins
- toaster oven

- Guide kids to wash their hands.
- Comment that Jesus had a special meal with His disciples.
- Remind kids that Jesus wants people to remember Him.
- Direct kids to mix food color into the bowls of milk.
- Encourage them to use pastry brushes to lightly "paint" their bread with the colored milk.
- Toast the bread on a light setting.
- Pour juice into each cup. Spread butter on the toast if desired and invite kids to enjoy the meal.
- Tell the Bible story "Jesus' Special Supper" (Matthew 26:17-30).
- Mention that some people at church take part in a special meal during worship called the Lord's Supper. During this special meal, people pray and remember what Jesus did. Everyone can think about Jesus and remember what He did.

CHANGE IT UP!

- God Sent the People Food (Exodus 16:1-18)
- God cares for people's needs.

- Jesus Made Breakfast for His Disciples (John 21:1-17)
- Jesus performed miracles and healed the sick.

- Ruth's Family (Ruth 1:22; 2:1-23)
- God wants families to love one another.

CHRUCH

Absolutely You Could ...
Thought-Igniting Ideas Why Maybe You Shouldn't!

I remember when God called me into full-time service to preschoolers. My husband and I were blessed with two children—only 13 months apart. We were members of a small congregation with no Sunday school class or program for toddlers. I heard a still small voice speaking to my heart:

You could keep them with you and hope they'll get something from the adult class ... but why would you?
I received blessings from the pastor and began a class for toddlers—mine. Soon I had four other preschoolers in the class, then my sister-in-law had twins. Talk about exponential growth! I watched as the youngest children participated in finger-plays, joining their tiny hands together to pray, sing and repeat simple Bible phrases. Jesus said, "Let the little children come to Me" (Mark 10:14). I was hooked!

You could cross your fingers and hope for the best ... but why would you?
Pray intentionally. Here's an example of my prayer schedule: Monday: Children and their parents; Tuesday: Younger Preschool volunteers; Wednesday: Younger Preschool leaders; Thursday: Sunday School teachers; Friday: Church staff; Saturday: Everyone—for good health, peace, and unity. Pray for God's protection and for His presence to be manifested in each person. Praying ensures that I arrive at church with anticipation—not wishful thinking (Philippians 4:6).

You could arrive frazzled ... but why would you?
Add value to your ministry and your sanity by planning ahead. Encourage volunteers to be prepared and on time. Ask God to turn your anxiety into confidence, and be strengthened with power through His Spirit (Ephesians 3:16). Children and volunteers feel more secure with a confident, organized leader.

You could pop in a video ... but why would you?
You have the great privilege and responsibility to make sure God's Word is being taught in each classroom. Display Bibles and provide Bible-based,

age-appropriate curriculum. Preschoolers will learn who God is and that His Word is special. Stress the importance of having a Bible story time, activities, games, and songs to teach Bible truths. Teach God's truths as you sit, as you walk, as you lie down, and as you get up (Deuteronomy 11:19). You're imparting truth and building a foundation of faith that can last into eternity.

You could be a "one man show" ... but why would you?
Building a team strengthens the ministry. Make recruitment a priority. Assess the gifts of your volunteers and delegate responsibilities. Assign positions according to each person's God-given gifts and talents.

You could listen to what people say ... but why would you?
Words can be discouraging! (See Proverbs 15:2.) Over time, comments such as "I couldn't do your job," or "I would love to help you out with younger preschoolers, but I need to be 'fed,'" can wear you down. God's Word will lift you up. Be diligent to present yourself approved to God, a worker who doesn't need to be ashamed, correctly teaching the word of truth (2 Timothy 2:15). God can turn a program into a vibrant ministry where people are placed on a waiting list to serve!

You could give up and quit ... but why would you?
During tough times, remember this Scripture: "Therefore, my dear brothers, be steadfast, immovable, always excelling in the Lord's work, knowing that your labor in the Lord is not in vain." (1 Corinthians 15:58) Today, I'm a grandmother and serve on a church staff. I still love to slip into the toddler class, get on the floor, and sing a fun song. Recently after such a moment, it took a little longer to raise myself up off the floor, and we all began to laugh. The teacher said, "You know, we could say we are too old for teaching preschoolers." Still giggling, I replied, "Yes, we could ... but why would we?"

Kathy Martin

CHAPTER 8
Community & World

109

About the LOBL Concept Area: Community & World

One Sunday the 4-year-old class role-played veterinarians; they took care of stuffed animals. That day one child's family joined the church. As the teacher greeted the family after the service, the little girl whispered, "How are the animals?"

What had she learned in Sunday School? Among other things, she heard that God gives people different work to do, and she practiced compassion.

Preschoolers are beginning to understand that other people have wants and needs. As they role-play taking care of sick people, preparing meals for friends, bathing a baby, or bringing food for the food bank, reinforce with conversation that they can help others.

As they build with blocks and paint murals, kids learn that God wants people to work together. They learn to consider others by taking turns using crayons, digging in sand, or leading a parade. They build communities with blocks and drive toy cars through the streets. They learn to show love and kindness to people.

Looking at maps or a globe shows kids that the world is big and they can care for people in other places. Teach them about missionary kids, what their lives are like in different parts of the world, and what they pray about. (See *www.kidsonmission.org*.) Kids can pray for and support missionaries.

Helen Owens

Important Note About Allergies:

When working with preschoolers it is important to always be aware of allergies. When using this book in a classroom setting, please print the allergy alert from the CD-ROM and inform parents of ingredients or nature items used in the activity.

SCIENCE & Nature

Collect Fingerprints

Invite kids to choose a stamp pad and make several of their own fingerprints on an index card. Write each child's name on his card when he begins the activity.

After stamping her own fingerprints, each child may ask friends to add fingerprints on the card too.

Talk with kids about things they enjoy doing with friends.

Share "David's Friend Jonathan" (1 Samuel 18:1-5).

Remind kids to thank God for friends to love. Provide wet wipes for cleanup.

- washable markers
- washable stamp pads
- 5-by-8-inch blank index cards
- wet wipes

CHANGE IT UP!

- The Wise Men Visited Jesus (Matthew 2:1-12)
- God sent Jesus to earth because He loves people.
- Use fingerprints to make figures of the wise men.

- Psalm 139:14
- Write the suggested verse on each child's card.

- God Created Man and Woman (Genesis 2:7–3:23)
- God created the earth and everything in it.

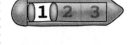

See Friends in a Mirror

- mirror

- Seat babies in front of a mirror so they can see each other.
- Talk about friends at church. Mention that teachers love babies and care about them.
- Wave to babies and encourage them to wave back.
- Talk to each baby. Tell her that the Bible tells about Jesus eating with His friend Matthew. Jesus loved His friends.

Pack a Suitcase

- small suitcase
- assorted clothing

- As a child packs the suitcase, talk about trips you have taken or the child has taken. Mention packing a Bible to read while you are traveling.
- Share the Bible story "People Welcomed Jesus" (Matthew 21:1-11, 14-16). Tell the child that when Jesus traveled to Jerusalem, the people welcomed Him.

Carry Doll in a Blanket

- baby doll
- small blanket

- Place the items on the floor. Invite two kids to put the doll on the blanket and each carry one side of the blanket.
- As kids work together, talk about the four friends who carried their friend who could not walk (Mark 2:1-12). The friends worked together. Point out that the kids are working together too.
- Talk about ways children can help each other.

ort Play Money

Fill an old handbag with play money, including coins.
Invite kids to sort the money into the different sections of
the egg carton.
Tell the Bible story "Jesus Showed Love to Zacchaeus"
(Luke 19:1-10).
Mention that Zacchaeus learned from Jesus about God and
His love. He gave money back to the people after he met Jesus.
God wants everyone to know about His love.

- play money
- egg carton
- old handbag

CHANGE IT UP!

- Ruth Took Care of Her Family (Ruth 1:22; 2:1-23)
- God wants family members to love one another.

- The Good Samaritan (Luke 10:25-37)
- God wants people to be kind and helpful.

- A Woman Gave an Offering (Mark 12:41-44)
- At church people have different kinds of jobs.

Help at Church

- Invite kids to play with the provided items and pretend they are helping at church.
- Open the Bible to Philippians 2:4 and read the verse, "Think about others before yourself." Explain that there are many helpers in church who put others first.
- Ask kids to name some church helpers. Look for pictures of church staff, custodians, and teachers in a church directory. Encourage kids to think of ways they can help at church.
- Ask boys and girls how they can put others first. Listen for ideas such as praying, sharing, cleaning up, and giving at church.

CHANGE IT UP!

- Jesus Fed the People (John 6:1-13)
- Jesus showed love by helping people.

- Paul Wrote God's Words in the Bible (Acts 17:1-4; 1 Thessalonians 3:2,6-8,11-13; 4)
- People wrote God's words in the Bible.

- David Obeyed His Father (1 Samuel 16:11-12; 17:12-22)
- People's choices make them happy or sad.

DRAMATIC PLAY

- offering plate
- child-sized broom and dustpan
- old telephone
- plastic lawn mower
- kitchen apron
- hymnal
- church pictorial directory
- other church items

Grocery Store

Stack boxes on their sides for displaying grocery items. Guide kids to set up a grocery store by arranging the containers and setting up a checkout area. Kids may take turns stocking shelves, shopping, and working as cashiers and baggers.

- Tell kids the Bible story "The Church Chose Special Helpers" (Acts 6:1-7). Mention that people at church can help others. Talk about how the early church members shared their money and all they owned to help one another.
- Ask how people could use items in a grocery store to help others. Help kids understand that people at church can give food to people who need help.

CHANGE IT UP!

- Jesus Taught About God's Care (Matthew 5:1-2; 6:25-34)
- Jesus taught people what God is like.

- Ruth's Family (Ruth 1:22; 2:1-23)
- God wants family members to love one another.

- Abram and Lot (Genesis 13:1-12,14-18)
- God wants people to get along with their family members.

- plastic grocery cart
- small boxes or crates
- assorted empty food containers
- play cash register or calculator
- play money
- paper or cloth grocery bags

COMMUNITY & WORLD

DRAMATIC PLAY

- bandages
- play money
- digital camera and docking station
- "Bible Times Clothing" (CD-ROM)—Follow the instructions to make Bible times clothing for kids.

The Good Samaritan in Action

- Invite kids to dress up in the Bible times clothing and play out the Bible story.
- Briefly tell "The Good Samaritan" (Luke 10:25-37). Then assign roles such as man who was robbed, priest, Levite, Samaritan, donkey, and innkeeper.
- Open the Bible to Luke 10:25-37 and read the story aloud. Ask kids to play out their roles (using the bandages and money) as they listen to the story.
- Enlist another adult to take four to five different pictures of the children as they play out the story.
- Print the pictures. Lead kids to examine the pictures and arrange them in sequential order.
- Allow kids to change roles and play out the story again. Encourage one child to tell the story in his own words as his friends play it out.

CHANGE IT UP!

JESUS

- Jesus Healed a Man Who Couldn't Hear (Mark 7:31-37)
- Jesus performed miracles and healed the sick.
- Follow the directions above to help preschoolers play out the story.

Bible

- Jeremiah Wrote About God (Jeremiah 36:1-4)
- People wrote God's words in the Bible.
- Follow the directions above to help preschoolers play out the story.

Self

- David, the Chosen King (1 Samuel 16:1-13)
- God has a plan for people.
- Follow the directions above to help preschoolers play out the story.

Friends Quilt

Cut the poster board into 8-inch squares. Punch holes in the corners of each square.

Give each child a poster board square. Invite him to draw a picture of himself and write his name (or let you write it). Allow kids to decorate their squares as they choose. Let them help you lay out the squares.

Use lengths of yarn to tie all the squares together to make a class quilt. Hang it in the room.

Tell the Bible story "Paul's Friends" (Acts 18:1-4,18-28) while kids work.

• Encourage the friends to thank God for one another.

- poster board
- scissors
- washable markers
- hole punch
- yarn

CHANGE IT UP!

- God Gave Rules to the People (Exodus 19:1–20:21)
- People show love for God by obeying Him.
- Follow the directions above but write the numbers *1-10* on each quilt piece.

- Jesus Was Born (Luke 2:1-20)
- God sent Jesus to earth because He loves people.
- Follow the directions above but draw a picture from the manger scene on each quilt piece.

- David and Jonathan (1 Samuel 14:49; 18:1-4; 20)
- People's choices can make them happy or sad.
- Follow the directions above but draw pictures from the Bible story on each quilt piece

- several Bibles
- tote bags or shoe boxes

Mini Messengers

- Invite kids to pretend to be messengers. Guide them to pack the Bibles into tote bags or boxes and deliver them to their friends around the room.
- Open your Bible to Mark 16:15 and read the verse aloud. Tell kids that God wants them to tell others about Jesus.
- Explain that missionaries help people by giving them Bibles and telling them about Jesus.

ξ CHANGE IT UP!

- Shepherds Visited Jesus (Luke 2:14-20)
- Shepherds told people about Jesus.

- Andrew Told His Brother About Jesus (John 1:35-42)
- Missionaries tell people about God and Jesus.

- Apollos Learned About Jesus (Acts 18:1-4,18-28)
- Church helpers teach about God and Jesus.

Music & Books

Go Tell It!

- Make a spinner by gluing a set of game cards onto heavyweight paper. Cut an arrow from another piece of paper. Push a brad through the arrow and the spinner. Loosen the brad enough for the arrow to spin around.
- Invite kids to take turns spinning the spinner.
- Guide kids to play the game. When the spinner stops, kids will describe a way they can tell about Jesus using the item in the picture, or describe what they can say at the place in the picture.
- Remind kids that God wants people at church to tell others about Jesus. Kids can tell others what they learn at church about Jesus.

CHANGE IT UP!

- Peter and Cornelius (Acts 10:1-33)
- God shows His love to all people.

- Jeremiah Wrote About God (Jeremiah 36:1-4)
- People wrote God's words in the Bible.

- The People Worshiped God (2 Chronicles 3:1-3; 5:1-3,11-13)
- People at church worship, pray, give, sing, read the Bible, and listen to teaching and preaching.

- scissors
- heavyweight paper
- brad
- "Spin and Tell Game Cards" (CD-ROM)— Cut apart. Glue one set to the spinner.

CHURCH

SCIENCE & Nature

- plastic dishpans
- large towel for cleanup
- small buckets or containers
- sponges of various sizes and textures

Move Water with Sponges

- Place two small buckets in each dishpan. Fill one of the buckets with water.
- Encourage each preschooler to choose a teammate to work with her. Give each child a sponge that fits easily into the buckets.
- Guide each pair to work together to move the water by soaking up the water in one bucket with sponges and squeezing it into the other bucket.
- Let preschoolers experiment with different sizes and textures of sponges.
- As preschoolers play, tell the Bible story "Aquila and Priscilla" (Acts 18:1-4,18-28). Tell kids that God wants people to work together.

 CHANGE IT UP!

- The People Crossed the Jordan River (Joshua 3–4)
- God shows His love to all people.

- Jesus and the Woman at the Well (John 4:6-11,19-30,39-42)
- Jesus taught people what God is like.

- God Created the World (Genesis 1:1–2:3)
- God created the earth and everything in it.

Fun and Exciting Holiday Celebrations with Kids

Ah, the holidays … cookies, candies, bunnies, baskets, stockings, and plump men in red suits; does it get any better than that? It does and it should! As a parent or teacher of preschoolers it's easy to get so caught up in the "fun" of the holidays that you miss the point. It's the "point" that is the really fun part!

Introducing preschoolers to the wonder of God's Word through holidays like Christmas and Easter should be exciting. But it's easy to let other things occupy your attention. Maybe you don't feel equipped to teach, or you think someone else will take responsibility, or maybe you don't realize how important celebrating the holidays really is. All excuses aside, it's time to discover the joy of celebrating the holidays with kids.

For Parents—How can you best celebrate the holidays with your preschoolers? First things first: keep it simple! Don't try to do everything … that's impossible! It's OK to say "no" to some events and activities.

Look for opportunities to introduce the truth of the holiday. Be careful where you place your emphasis. Don't get so wrapped up with Santa or the Easter bunny that you miss teaching your kids the truth about Christmas and Easter. Look for ways to focus on Jesus and God's love for people. At Christmas, talk about the wise men following the star as you hang Christmas lights, or turn off the lights and sing Christmas carols around the Christmas tree.

At Easter, plant flowers and talk about how much Jesus loves people, or make a magazine picture collage of people to remind your child that Jesus loves everyone. Focus your child (and yourself) on what the holiday is really all about.

Another way to celebrate is through traditions. Preschoolers love repetition. It's the way they learn best, and it is also a source of comfort. Create some wonderful Christmas traditions with your child—put up a new piece of the nativity scene in each week of December, decorate cupcakes and deliver them to a nursing home, read the Christmas story from Luke on Christmas Eve, or make homemade wrapping paper by stamping with star-shaped cookie cutters onto brown paper. Easter traditions could include making J-shaped sugar cookies and taking them to people who are homebound, donating and planting flowers at your church, or singing songs about Jesus on Easter morning. Traditions don't have to be elaborate, but they should be thoughtful.

The most important thing to remember is "quality of time." Don't let the season be filled with hustle and bustle. Focus on spending time with your child; talk about or do activities that will point him to the true meaning of the holiday!

For Teachers—Teachers have the not-so-simple task of trying to combat the images of Christmas and Easter that preschoolers see everywhere in their world and showing them the true meaning of the holidays.

As a teacher, you have only a short opportunity each week with the kids you teach. Out of 168 hours in a week, you will probably spend no more than 2 hours with your group of preschoolers. So what will you fill that time with?

Consider this: preschoolers think in literal terms; they cannot easily distinguish between fantasy and reality. What are the kids in your class seeing and hearing during the holiday season? Are there images of Baby Jesus mixed with visions of men in red suits or flying reindeer? Be thoughtful about what you bring to your class. Don't send mixed messages to your preschoolers. They're getting mixed messages everywhere they go! Let church be the place they can come and hear the truth. You only have a short time with them, so make it count!

Jennfier Cogley

Important Note About Allergies:

When working with preschoolers it is important to always be aware of allergies. When using this book in a classroom setting, please print the allergy alert from the CD-ROM and inform parents of ingredients or nature items used in the activity.

Make Christmas Cards

- old Christmas cards
- glue
- scissors
- construction paper
- markers
- stickers
- gold- or silver-colored ribbon

- Gather old Christmas cards that show biblical pictures of Christmas.
- Organize materials on the table.
- Invite kids to use the materials to make Christmas cards. Kids may cut and glue parts of the old cards to a folded piece of construction paper. Tell the Bible story "Jesus Will Be Born" (Matthew 1:18-25; Luke 1:26-56) as they work.
- Write out Luke 1:31 on each child's card. Read the verse aloud with him.
- Remind kids that God chose Mary, Joseph, and Jesus to be a family. Tell them that sharing their cards with friends is one way they can tell others this good news.

Sponge Paint Gift Wrap Paper

- paint
- aluminum pan
- painting smocks
- sponge shapes (stars, hearts)
- large sheets of paper or newsprint

- Spread the painting materials on a table. Pour a thin layer of paint in the aluminum pan.
- Lead each child to dip a sponge shape in the paint and stamp it on his paper.
- As kids work, tell the Bible story "Wise Men Worshiped Jesus" (Matthew 2:1-12). Emphasize that the wise men bowed before Jesus and gave gifts to Jesus as they worshiped Him.
- Demonstrate how to bow and encourage kids to bow.
- Encourage kids to use the painted paper as gift wrap.

Make a Starry Night Picture

SCIENCE & Nature

- Make a star gazer by using a pencil to poke holes in black construction paper. Use a rubber band to position the paper over the light end of a flashlight.
- Tell kids the Bible story "The Wise Men Visited Jesus" (Matthew 2:1-12). Invite kids to see what a starry night might be like.
- Turn off the overhead lights. Shine the flashlight at the ceiling so kids can see the "stars." Ask kids how the wise men found Jesus. (*They followed a bright star.*)
- Turn on the lights. Invite each child to make a starry night picture using black construction paper, white crayons, and star stickers.
- As kids work, remind them that the wise men followed the star to Jesus so they could worship Him.
- Encourage kids to count their stars when they are finished. Allow them to put several star stickers together to make one star "brighter" than the others to match the Bible story.

- flashlight
- pencil
- rubber band
- white crayons
- black construction paper
- star stickers

Good Thinking

Puzzles & MANIPULATIVES

- Explain that each card in the stack has two pictures on it. The goal is to turn over two Good Thinking squares that match the pictures on the card (not necessarily two matching "squares").
- Turn over a card, then guide a child to turn over two squares. If the revealed squares do not match the pictures on the card, move the card to the bottom of the stack and guide the child to return the squares. Then allow another child to take a turn.
- Use the pictures on the cards as a prompt for telling key parts of the Bible story "Jesus Was Born" (Luke 2:1-20).
- Remind kids that the shepherds heard the good news of Jesus' birth. They went back to their sheep, praising and thanking God for Jesus.

- "Good Thinking Cards" (CD-ROM)— Cut apart and stack cards facedown on a table.
- "Good Thinking Squares" (CD-ROM)— Cut apart. Arrange cards facedown in a 5-by-5 grid.

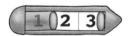

Build a Manger

- fresh hay, craft straw, or shredded brown paper
- small baby doll
- wooden building blocks
- animal figures or small stuffed animals
- large sheet for a floor covering
- picture of a manger or manger scene

- Spread out the sheet on the floor and place the items on it.
- As children investigate the items, tell them that after Jesus was born, Mary wrapped Him in strips of cloth and laid Him in a manger. Show the picture. Explain that a manger is a feeding box for animals.
- Suggest that they use the materials to build and arrange a manger. Ask: "Who did Mary lay in the manger?"
- Encourage kids to role-play Mary and Joseph or the shepherds visiting Baby Jesus.
- Open your Bible and read 1 John 4:10 aloud. Emphasize that God loves each person and sent His Son Jesus.

Create Sand Art

- transportation toys
- sand and water table or plastic tub—Fill with 2-3 inches of sanitized play sand.
- plastic floor covering such as a shower curtain
- books containing pictures of the wise men
- crayons, glue
- construction paper

- Display the pictures of the wise men. Arrange the tub of sand and transportation toys on the floor covering. Invite kids to explore the sand using the transportation toys. As kids play, read the Bible story "The Wise Men Visited Jesus" (Matthew 2:1-12). Emphasize that the wise men traveled to Jesus to worship Him.
- Invite kids to each make a sand art picture. Guide them to draw the wise men traveling. After they have finished their drawings, they can make a path with a thin line of glue and sprinkle sand over the glue.
- Explain that the Bible does not specifically describe how the wise men traveled, but they might have ridden camels on their journey across the desert.

Make a Christmas Garland

- Display the index cards. Guide kids to write the words on separate paper strips.
- Show kids how to pull together and tape the ends of a strip to form a loop. Repeat this, linking the loops together until they have formed a chain.
- Tell the Bible story "Jesus Was Born" (Luke 2:1-20). Remind kids that Christmas is the time people celebrate Jesus' birth.

- scissors
- markers
- clear tape
- red and green paper—Cut into 11-by-1-inch strips.
- index cards—Write the following words on separate cards: *Isaiah, angel, Mary, Joseph, Baby Jesus, shepherds, wise men, manger.*

All Wrapped Up

- Arrange the cloth strips next to the baby doll.
- Guide kids to swaddle the baby by wrapping the strips of cloth around the doll. To swaddle with the blanket, guide a child to place the blanket on a flat surface and fold down one of the top corners. Position the doll's head right above the fold. Pull one corner of the blanket across the doll's body and tuck it under the doll's back. Fold the opposite corner is over the doll's chest, then tuck the bottom triangle under the doll's chin.
- Tell kids that when Jesus was born, Mary wrapped Him in swaddling cloths.
- Show kids how to find the Book of Luke in the Bible. Show them the Old Testament and the New Testament.
- Comment that God sent Jesus to show people how much He loves them.

- cloth strips, bundling wrap, or baby blanket
- baby doll

DRAMATIC PLAY

- construction paper
- scissors
- tape
- plastic doll

Follow the Stars

- Cut several large stars from construction paper. Tape the stars to the floor throughout the classroom, making a long path. Position a doll at the end of the path.
- Encourage kids to hop from star to star, following the path to the doll.
- Comment that God provided a bright star so the wise men would know that God's Son was born.
- Tell the Bible story "The Wise Men Visited Jesus" (Matthew 2:1-12) as you allow kids to create new paths by rearranging the stars and doll. After a few rearrangements, suggest a path on the wall and lead kids to "hop" using their hands instead of their feet as they touch each star on the way to the doll.
- To review the story, ask kids what the wise men followed and what they gave Jesus.

SCIENCE & Nature

- bubble solution
- bubble wands
- small Christmas cookie cutters (such as star, bell, tree)
- pie pan

Bubble Shapes

- Position the pie pan with bubble solution in a safe place on the floor. Lay wands and cookie cutters beside the pie pan.
- Invite kids to experiment with the wands and cookie cutters to blow bubbles. Point out that no matter what shape is used, the bubbles are always round.
- Tell the Bible story "The Wise Men Visited Jesus" (Matthew 2:1-12). Ask kids what the wise men followed to find Jesus. Show the star cutter and comment that the wise men followed a star to Jesus. The wise men worshiped Jesus.
- Emphasize that the wise men recognized that Jesus was special and they gave him gifts as a way of worshiping Him. God sent His Son to show people how much He loves them.

Pack a Suitcase

- Invite a child to pack items in the suitcase as if he were going on a trip.
- Ask the child about trips he has taken with his family and what he packs. Mention that Mary and Joseph went on a trip to Bethlehem, the town where Jesus was born. Say that Jesus was born in Bethlehem.

- small suitcase or backpack
- child's pajamas
- plastic toothbrush holder
- empty shampoo bottle

Play with Farm Animals and Straw

- Guide kids to make a manger with the box and straw. Put the animals around the manger.
- Mention that animals might have been near the place where Mary cared for Baby Jesus. Tell kids that Jesus' birth was special.

- straw or shredded brown paper
- shallow box
- vinyl farm animals

Fill and Dump Gift Bags

- Put the items in the gift bags and set the bags on the floor.
- Watch a child dump the items on the floor then put them back in the bag. Mention that people often put gifts in bags.
- Remark that the Bible says that people were happy when Jesus was born. The wise men took special gifts to Jesus. At Christmas people give gifts to others because they love them.

- several gift bags
- small toys

Drive Toy Cars

- several toy cars and trucks
- a few small wrapped gift boxes

- Watch kids enjoy playing with the vehicles. If the trucks are large enough, suggest that kids load up the gifts to deliver to each other.
- As kids play, tell them the Bible story "The Wise Men Visited Jesus" (Matthew 2:1-12).

Play with Baby Items

- doll
- diaper bag filled with an assortment of baby items

- Invite kids to explore the contents of the diaper bag.
- Comment that parents use the items to take care of their baby. As kids play with the items, tell the Bible story "Jesus Was Born" (Luke 2:1-20). Emphasize that Mary and Joseph cared for Baby Jesus.

Make a Fabric Collage

- tape
- clear contact plastic
- 1- and 2-inch squares of soft baby fabric

- Tape the contact plastic to the wall or floor, sticky side out.
- Lead kids to make a collage on the sticky paper using the soft fabric.
- Tell the Bible story "Jesus Was Born" (Luke 2:1-20).
- Emphasize that Mary and Joseph loved Baby Jesus very much and took care of Him.

Make a Card for a Friend

Tell the Bible story "Jesus Is Alive" (John 20:1-18). Emphasize that Mary had good news to tell the disciples: Jesus is alive!
Help a child fold a piece of paper in fourths to make a card she can decorate. Help her "sound out" words she wants to spell or write the words on paper for her to copy.
- Demonstrate how to put the card in an envelope and "stamp" it with a sticker.
- Comment that Jesus' disciples were happy to hear Mary say, "Jesus is alive!" Point out that people are happy when they hear good news.

- assorted colors of copy paper
- washable markers
- stickers
- envelopes

Phone the Good News

- Tell the Bible story "Jesus Is Alive" (John 20:1-18). Emphasize that Mary had good news to tell the disciples: Jesus is alive!
- Show kids how to use tape to secure the string tightly between the cups and take turns talking or listening. Comment that people use their voices and ears to talk and listen about good news. Encourage kids to "call" each other and say, "Jesus is alive!"
- Remark that Jesus is God's Son. Tell kids they can call their friends and tell them that Jesus died on the cross but now He is alive!

- paper cups
- string
- tape

Make a Class Poster

- poster board
- scissors
- washable markers
- glue sticks
- kid-friendly magazines

- Before class, write *Jesus Is Alive!* on the poster board.
- Guide kids to look through the magazines and cut out pictures of smiling faces. Direct them to glue the faces to the poster board. As they work, announce that today they are celebrating that Jesus is alive. Comment that Mary was so happy when she saw Jesus in the garden that she ran to tell Jesus' disciples.
- Tell the Bible story "Jesus Is Alive" (John 20:1-18). Point out that at first, Mary did not know what had happened to Jesus' body. It was supposed to be in the tomb; but when Mary got there, the tomb was empty. Tell kids that this made Mary sad because she thought someone had stolen Jesus' body. But Mary was happy when she talked to Jesus. Jesus is alive!

Create a Flower Garden Picture

- green strips of paper
- large sheets of construction paper
- pastel-colored paper muffin cups and mini muffin cups
- glue, washable markers, scissors

- Guide each child to design a flower garden on a sheet of paper by gluing muffin cups for flowers and green strips of paper for stems.
- Allow kids to decide how many "flowers" to make and to arrange them in any way they choose. Invite kids to use the markers to draw other things in their gardens.
- Use John 20:1-18 and Mark 16:1-8 to tell about Mary's visit to the garden. Emphasize that when Mary left the garden, she was happy because she knew Jesus is alive.
- Explain that Easter is a happy time when kids can remember that Jesus is alive and He loves them.

Play with Alphabet Blocks

Write the names *Mary* and *Jesus* in large letters on paper. Place the paper and alphabet blocks on a table. Invite kids to sort the letter blocks they know and find the alphabet blocks to spell their names. Then help kids spell the names *Jesus* and *Mary* using the written words as a guide.

- Comment that the Bible tells that Jesus is God's Son. Add that the Bible also says that Jesus is alive and He loves all people.
- Write the phrase *Jesus Is Alive!* on the paper and challenge kids to spell it with blocks.

- alphabet blocks (or alphabet foam letters, or plastic magnetic letters and cookie sheet)
- paper
- washable marker

Create a Necklace

- Position the items on the table. Tell the Bible story "Jesus Is Alive" (John 20:1-18). Emphasize that the women found the stone rolled away.
- Invite kids to create necklaces. Demonstrate wrapping a chenille stem around a stone. Wrap it up, down, and across so the stone will not slip out. Twist then tuck in the ends. Guide each child to do the same.
- Measure a 24-inch length of lacing for each child and ask him to cut it. Show him how to slide the lacing under the wrapped chenille stem. Make sure the necklace fits over the child's head before forming a knot.
- Comment: "When a friend asks you why you have a stone around your neck, tell him it reminds you that the tomb was empty and Jesus is alive!"

- chenille stems
- small rocks
- plastic lacing or colored leather cord
- scissors

Prepare for an Easter Celebration

- place mats
- assorted dishes and plastic food
- flowers for centerpiece

- Talk with kids about family celebrations at Easter. Encourage boys and girls to play out preparing and eating a meal. Guide kids to set the table for a celebration.
- Tell elements of the Bible story "Jesus Is Alive" (John 20:1-18) as kids play. Assist boys and girls in opening their Bibles to Matthew 28:7 and reading "Jesus is alive."
- Share that people are happy and celebrate Easter because Jesus is alive.

Tear and Glue Paper

- white copy paper
- glue
- green construction paper

- Guide a child to tear green paper into pieces. Then she can glue the paper pieces onto a white piece of paper.
- Comment how the green paper resembles leaves. Remark that people waved green palm leaves to show love to Jesus.
- Say the Bible phrase, "People thanked God for Jesus." (Matthew 15:31)

Create with Sunrise Colors

- manila paper
- washable markers
- colored pencils and crayons in yellow, pink, light orange, and lilac

- Talk with kids about what the sky looks like when the sun comes up.
- Guide kids to create a morning sky with the art materials. Offer to write the Bible phrase, *Jesus Is Alive!* (Matthew 28:7), on a child's drawing.
- Comment that Mary went to the tomb early in the morning. Tell the Bible story "Jesus Is Alive" (John 20:1-18).

Phone Others to Tell About Jesus

Briefly tell the Bible story "Jesus Is Alive" (John 20:1-18) as kids play with the phones. Suggest that kids "call" friends or family members to tell them that the Bible says that Jesus is alive. "Phone" a child and have a conversation about Jesus to help reluctant boys and girls become involved in the play.

Talk about how happy people are to know that Jesus is alive and that He loves them. Say: "Jesus is alive!"

• toy phones

Play Step Bells

MuSic & BooKS

• Show kids how to use a mallet to play different notes on the bells and sing the words *Jesus is alive*. You might play the notes E, E, D, D, C or C#, E, G, E, C while you sing. Guide kids to make up their own tunes to sing about how Jesus is alive.
• Put colored sticky dots on the step bell bars, using a different color for each note. Provide paper and additional dots so kids can create a melody chart of the songs they create.
• Say: "Jesus is alive! Happy Easter!"

• colored sticky dots
• step bells
• mallet
• paper

Explore and Sort Rocks

SCIENCE & Nature

• Invite boys and girls to explore the rocks and sort them into shoe boxes according to their size, texture, color, or shape.
• Briefly tell the Bible story "Jesus Is Alive" (John 20:1-18) as kids sort. Emphasize that the stone had already been rolled away when Mary and the other women arrived at the tomb.
• Say: "Jesus is alive! Happy Easter!"

• magnifying glasses
• four shoe boxes
• rocks of different sizes, textures, colors, and shapes

Understanding Each Page

Each activity in this book is categorized by one of the Levels of Biblical Learning™ concept areas. For your convenience, each page is labeled with a helpful tab that indicates the concept area for which the activity is written.

For ease of use, the prep steps for each activity conveniently located in the margin.

SUPER DUPER: CHAPTER 4

Sandstorm Creations

- plastic tablecloth
- masking tape
- funnel
- tub of sand
- twine or heavy string
- scoop or spoon
- ice pick (teacher use)

- Spread a plastic tablecloth across the floor and tape down the edges.
- Use an ice pick to poke three evenly-spaced holes around the rim of a large funnel.
- Loop twine through the holes and gather the ends together so the funnel will hang evenly.
- Hang the funnel from the ceiling and position it several inches above the ground.
- Place a tub of sand, a scoop, a broom, and a dustpan on the tablecloth.
- Demonstrate how to scoop sand into the funnel and gently swing the twine to make designs on the tablecloth.
- Encourage kids to use the scoops to pour sand into the funnel. Allow them to make designs on the tablecloth by gently moving the funnel as the sand escapes. Sweep up the sand design and return sand to the tub before the next person's turn.
- Guide kids to take turns forming things God created.
- Share "God Made the World" (Genesis 1:1–2:3). Remind kids that God made the world and everything in it.

CHANGE IT UP! This book was designed with practicality in mind. When you use this book, you'll notice a **CHANGE IT UP!** icon at the bottom of each activity. The **CHANGE IT UP!** icon gives you an opportunity to modify the activity to fit a different LOBL concept area.

Look at the "Sandstorm Creation" activity example above. This activity was originally written for the LOBL concept area of *Creation*, but can be easily modified to fit the LOBL concept areas of *God*, *Jesus*, or *Family*.

CHANGE IT UP!

- God Helped the People (Exodus 12–16)
- God is real. God can do all things.

- Jesus and the Woman at the Well (John 4:6-11,19-30,39-42)
- Jesus taught people what God is like.

- Ruth Helped Her Family (Ruth 1:22; 2:1-23)
- God wants families to help each other.

Sometimes all you need to do is tell the suggested Bible story and replace the concept statement from the original activity. Other times, you might suggest that kids create drawings, sand creations, or so forth. The adaptations don't need to be complicated.

Here are some sample adaptations for "Sandstorm Creations" activity:
- **God:** Tell the suggested story. Encourage kids to draw sand pictures of helping a friend.
- **Jesus:** Tell the suggested story. Challenge kids to draw sand pictures of Jesus helping the woman. After the sand has emptied from the bag, let kids use their finger to draw pictures in the sand of people helping one another.
- **Family:** Tell the suggested story. Direct kids to draw sand pictures of their family members.

Make using this book fun for yourself and kids. Using the suggested LOBL adaptations creates an additional three activities on every page. That makes more than 400 activities in this book!

Foundational Bible Stories for Babies-Kindergartners

God Made the World and Everything In It . . . . Genesis 1:1–2:3

God Made Families . . . . Genesis 1:26-31; 2:7,15-24; 4:1-2

Noah and the Ark. . . . . Genesis 6:9-10,14-22; 7:1,13-19; 8:1-3,13-20; 9:12-16

Joseph . . . . Genesis 45:1-11,16-28; 46:26-34; 47:1-11

Miriam and Baby Moses . . . . Exodus 2:1-10

Ruth's Family . . . . .Ruth 1:22; 2:1-23

Hannah's Prayer and Boy Samuel . . . . 1 Samuel 1:1-28; 2:18-21,26

David Helped His Family . . . . 1 Samuel 16:11-12; 17:12-22

David and Jonathan . . . . 1 Samuel 14:49; 18:1-4; 20:4,17

God Helped Elijah . . . . 1 Kings 17:1-16

Elisha's Friends Helped. . . . . 2 Kings 4:8-13

Solomon and the Temple . . . . 2 Chronicles 3:1-17; 5:1-14

Daniel Obeyed God and Chose Good Food . . . . Daniel 1:1-20

Jesus' Birth and Related Events. . . . . Matthew 1:18-24; Luke 1:26-56; Luke 2:1-20; Matthew 2:1-12

SUPER DUPER TOPICAL INDEX

SCRIPTURE REFERENCES

. . . .

AGE LEVELS

CD-ROM Items

Activity Helps

Bible Stories

1. God Made the World and Everything In It
2. God Made Families
3. Noah and the Ark
4. Joseph
5. Miriam and Baby Moses
6. Ruth's Family
7. Hannah's Prayer and Boy Samuel
8. David Helped His Family
9. David and Jonathan
10. Solomon and the Temple
11. God Helped Elijah
12. Elisha's Friends Helped
13. Daniel Obeyed God and Chose Good Food
14. Jesus' Birth and Related Events
15. Jesus Went to Church
16. Jesus Chose Special Helpers
17. Four Friends Who Helped
18. Jesus Fed the People
19. A Woman Gave Her Money
20. The Good Samaritan
21. Jesus Visited Mary and Martha
22. The Man Who Said Thank You
23. Zacchaeus Met Jesus
24. Jesus and the Children
25. Jesus Talked to the Woman at the Well
26. The Triumphal Entry
27. Jesus Is Alive!
28. Breakfast with Jesus
29. Philip and the Ethiopian
30. Timothy Learned About God
31. Paul Taught Lydia About Jesus

Training Plans

1. Super Duper Bible Skills for Preschoolers
2. Thought-Igniting Words Preschoolers Understand
3. The Super Duper Mind-Body Learning Connection
4. Super Duper Somethings from Almost Absolutely Nothing
5. Preparing Your Child for Thought-Igniting Learning
6. Igniting & Exciting Ways to Guide Behavior
7. Absolutely You Could … Thought-Igniting Ideas Why Maybe You Shouldn't!
8. Fun and Exciting Holiday Celebrations with Kids

Other Resources

1. Allergy Alert
2. Levels of Biblical Learning™
3. Alphabet Recipes
4. More Games for Preschoolers

9667832R0

FURTHER RECOMMENDATIONS: KNOWLEDGE IS POWER

http://www.shazzie.com/life/articles/raw_vegan_children.shtml

Your Right To Know: Genetic Engineering and the Secret Changes in Your Food, by Andrew Kimball

Food Inc, documentary film. Magnolia Home Entertainment www.foodincmovie.com

Food Matters, documentary film. Permacology Productions www.foodmatters.tv

The GMO Trilogy, documentary film. DENKmal-Films & Haifisch Films www.seedsofdeception.com

Organic Foods Production Act of 1990: http://www.ams.usda.gov/AMSv1.0/getfile?dDocNam e=STELPRDC5060370&acct=nopgeninfo

USDA National Organic Program Website: http://www.ams.usda.gov/AMSv1.0/nop

REFERENCES

Database on NOSB Recommendations for Materials Considered for Use in Organic Agricultural Production and Handling (XLS). 8/28/2010. http://www.ams.usda.gov/AMSv1.0/ getfile?dDocName=STELDEV3100278&acct=nopgeninfo

Kimball, Andrew. *Your Right To Know: Genetic Engineering and the Secret Changes in Your Food.* San Rafael, CA: Earth Awareness Editions, 2007.

Macisco, Debra, Master of Science, Acupuncture and Chinese Medicine. Advisory meeting. Ensenada, Mexico, 9/6/2010

Pitchford, Paul. *Healing With Whole Foods: Asian Traditions and Modern Nutrition.* Berkley, CA: North Atlantic Books, 1992.

Soria, Cherie. Class lectures. Living Light Institute, Fort Bragg, CA. April 2009

Cousens,Gabriel M.D *Conscious Eating* Berkley, CA: North Atlantic Books, First printing 2000

Organic Foods Production Act of 1990. 9/4/2010, http://www.ams.usda.gov/AMSv1.0/getfile? dDocName=STELPRDC5060370&acct=nopgeninfo

Gates, Donna. *The Body Ecology Diet, 10th edition.* Bogart, GA. B.E.D. Publications, 2007.